It's All
About
Attitude

It's All About Attitude

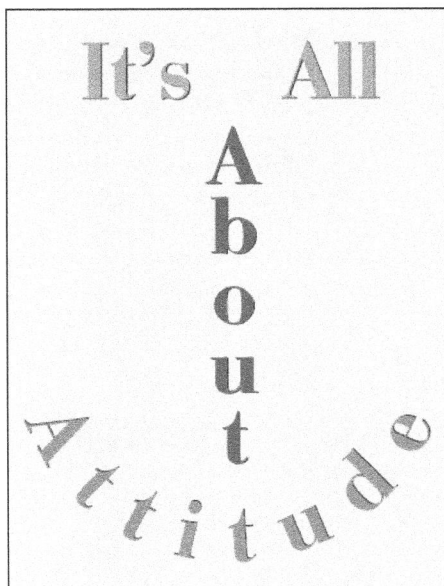

Finding the Strength to Survive

Alys Capozzi

FCP

Full Court Press
Englewood Cliffs, New Jersey

First Edition

Copyright © 2013 by Alys Capozzi

Published in the United States of America
by Full Court Press, 601 Palisade Avenue
Englewood Cliffs, NJ 07632
www.fullcourtpressnj.com

Some of the names in this book have been changed
to protect the privacy of individuals.

ISBN 978-1-938812-10-1
Library of Congress Control No. 2013935473

*Editing and Book Design by Barry Sheinkopf
for Bookshapers (www.bookshapers.com)*

Colophon by Liz Sedlack

TO MY SON, TRISTIAN
who has taught me more about life
by being a part of mine

ACKNOWLEDGMENTS

This book would not have been possible without the help of my beautiful child, Tristian Capozzi, who inspires me to follow my visions when I mention them to him. Together with my mother, Nilda Travieso, they have supported me and encouraged me to fulfill my dreams. I wouldn't have done this without additional help from my sister, Nilda Roos, my lovely niece, Hanna Roos, and my husband, Richard Capozzi. Thanks as well to the friends that remained my friends through difficult times.

I am grateful to the many physicians who have been a part of my many years of battle with illnesses—in particular, Dr. Adolfo Millan, Dr. William Sheramata, Dr. Janice Maldonado, and Dr. Marco Maldonado; to Dr. Pliskow for the easy access I had to him during my nerve-wracking pregnancy; and to any other physicians I may have failed to mention. Thank you to my physical therapist, Jim Thomaselli, too, for encouraging me to move!

A special thank-you as well to all the teachers who have been a part of Tristian's education. He learned from each of them.

I cannot complete my acknowledgments without mentioning my editor, Barry Sheinkopf. I appreciate the guidance he has given me on how to write this book. I'm grateful I was given his name by my friend, Julia Torres.

And thanks, finally, to Andrew Marra, of the *Palm Beach Post*, for initially helping me to start this vision. I told you, Andy—"I am going to do this!"

The Journey

(December 1992)

How do you know where to go?
Are you searching for answers
at the end of a rainbow?
Was it what you expected
once you got there ?
Or do you think life's unfair?
Perhaps you've been looking through
Rose-colored glasses,
Hoping this bad time eventually passes.
Did you honestly think
you would never feel sorrow?
Did you really believe
in just happy tomorrows?
Not once were you told
That this would be easy
That prediction you made on your own.
Seldom does life ever go as expected.
But find comfort in knowing,
That you're not alone.
I wish I had answers
to life's many questions,
But sadly, I can't say I do.
All I can say is

I live day to day,
Knowing eventually
I'll find the way.

Introduction

I wish there were a book, a guide, instruction manual, *something*, to guide me through this situation called Life. It's quite challenging at best. So I tell myself, "Don't just wish it, do it!" I tell others, "Watch me. Learn from me." Life can be as difficult or as rewarding as you choose. It's up to you. Control that which can. There are going to be events you are faced with over which you have no control. Make all of it bearable on yourself; take charge of what you can. What do I know? Hey, I'm just doing what I can to survive.

I was born in sunny South Florida in 1966. I resembled a Chinese baby with narrow eyes (thanks to my Chinese great-great-grandfather) and lots of straight, dark-brown hair. I was a big, healthy baby girl, over nine pounds. I was born seven years after my older sister. My life began following the departure of my parents and older sister, who was nine months old at the time, from Cuba. They left the island in 1960, just as Fidel Castro was taking control of it. I now know how fortunate I was to have been given life in this country. I am free to be me.

During my unpredictable, challenging times (there have been way too many of them), I have faced situations in which I have just wanted to give up—when I learned how difficult it is to do what is right. I've found making the easy choice often turns out to be the wrong one. I've learned how rewarding, how truly awesome, it feels when I make the right decision instead. It takes strength you never heard of or knew you had. *That's* life. You can't say you weren't warned. So put on your seatbelt: Success requires safety.

It sounds good, anyway. I sound *sooo* wise. Where was this wisdom when I was growing up? Where were the people who claimed to be there for me? Everybody has something. I mean, we all encounter situations we think we can't handle. Whether it's job loss, illness, loss of a loved one, it's *all the same.* The pain we feel, it's *all the same.* We think no one can know what we are feeling, but it's *all the same.* That's what they taught us when I was being trained to volunteer at The Crisis Line. I wanted to help others, so I chose to become a nurse. Surprise! This life thing took another bite out of plans I made years ago, before I learned that life seldom goes as we plan. I indeed became an R.N. at nineteen, but after that, *wow!* I learned to stop expecting things to go as planned, and to pray for the strength to deal with whatever confronts me. I am often asked, "How do you do it? How can you sit there with a smile on your face?"

I answer, "What are my choices? I can laugh, cr I can cry. Laughing, smiling, has given me—and others who speak to me—much better results. This is my story. This is how *I* managed to do it. I want to share what it is with whoever might be asking, *Why is this happening to me?*

—A.C.

I hope this journal is as good of a friend to you as mine is to me. It's the only place you can escape to where noone can find you. Whenever you're depressed and noone seems to care, come here to escape. And when things are perfect, come here to celebrate. Sometimes this journal will seem like your only friend. Other times, you won't even think about writing in it. But, you'll know it's there when you need to get away.

My sister's inscription in the journal she gave me—my
first—for Christmas in 1981

1

The Early (Easy) Years

December 25, 1981

I had the merriest Christmas this year. My grandmother left to return to Cuba after visiting us for a few weeks. I got to meet her for the first time. She resembles my mom with dark brown shoulder length hair and dark brown eyes. She is a spunky, petite ball of energy! I am grateful to have been given the opportunity to see who my mother had as an example for being a mom. You know how Christmas is about love, and it's the time of year to put your troubles aside to celebrate? That's what this year was like. I felt really close to everyone around me. I mean, why shouldn't I, right? I have a super best friend, my sister and I get along great, I got everything I asked for, and I didn't have one let down today. *I want every day to be like today.*

December 26, 1981

I just had to write about how happy I am. Today I spent most of the day putting my Lancerette scrapbook together, the Lancerettes Drill Team for John I. Leonard High School. So far this year, we have won a trophy for our routine at camp. We perform pre-game for our home football games, half-time for homecoming, and at pep rallies as well. We also march in parades. I am a sophomore this year.

I had a long talk this evening with my mother and stepfather, Raul, not about anything in particular—it was so nice. I haven't talked to them this way in a long time. I mean really *talked*, not just good morning, good night, hello, or goodbye. Anyway, I just wanted to write it down so I'll remember what Raul said. He told me, with a smile on his face, "*No lo pierde*," which is Spanish for "Don't lose it."

I guess he was talking about just being happy and satisfied with Life. I'm going to remember that.

January 4, 1982

I went back to school today after two weeks of vacation. I slept so badly last night, I was so sleepy today. We finally got our calendars at Lancerette practice. We made calendars featuring us for a fundraiser. We could have done a car wash. Oh, yeah, we did that, too!

January 19, 1982

At practice today, we discussed competition. We decided *not* to go to Dallas for National Competition. Instead, we are going to State Competition. We don't have enough money, or time, for fundraisers. Also we were put in groups for our Lancerette Show, *Lancerettes Live*, to raise more money.

January 10, 1982

We performed at the basketball game Friday night, playing against Forest Hill High School. I only mention it because I saw a few friends from Meadow Park Elementary School. We were *cheerleaders* then. I don't remember getting as exhausted from cheerleading as I do now. I started to attend there in fourth grade. It was after my parents' divorce. Prior to that, I started kindergarten at Kirklane Elementary School, where I attended through third grade. I remember being hospitalized with thrombophlebitis (a blood clot) when I was in sixth grade. Other than that, I didn't get sick too often.

February 15, 1982

Lancerettes will be having a paid assembly after competition of *Lancerettes Live* to raise more money. On Friday the 12th we had a lot of problems with lights and music. It was my turn to say my lines, and just as I started, the lights went out! Everything worked out in the end, though. We had fun, anyway!

February 20, 1982

We performed at the pep rally and the football game for the last time this school year. I can't believe that was our last performance.

The 1983 John I. Leonard Award-Winning Lancerettes.
I am far right, back row.

March 1982

We left for competition on the 12th, came home with 1 Superior, and slept on the bus during the long way home. Everyone slept on the bus. It was fun but exhausting!

April 29, 1982

Lancerette tryouts have been going on the last few weeks for the next school year, my junior year. I made it, again! There are 20 members instead of 34, and Lancerette practice will be a *class* next year. We get *credit* for it! We are all going to be members of a Nautilus gym. This is the start of working out at a gym—for me, anyway.

May 29, 1982

I met a guy last night, a senior football player. (*He ended up being my boyfriend for too long. At that age, I should have been meeting different guys, dating some I already knew, learning how I should be treated, and how I should not tolerate being mistreated   I should have given myself permission to be with someone who respected me for being me.)*

June 15, 1982

I have been having some numbness on my entire left side. It feels like when you sleep too long in the same position and wake up with the side you were sleeping on is still sleeping! My mother and Raul took me to John F. Kennedy Hospital. We were there for three hours just to find out they didn't know what I had! We got home at 10:30 p.m. I studied for my final exams tomorrow.

On Wednesday afternoon, I spent the whole time going to Dr. Berger's office (a neurologist) about my numbness. Dr. Berger asked me, "Do you feel the quarter in the palm of your hand?"

"Yes, but I feel the one in my left hand less," I said.

Finally, Dr. Berger told me he thought it was just *nerves!* I thought, I suppose—I *am* taking finals.

Rick, my boyfriend, came over that night and asked me if I wanted to go to his Senior Class Night with him, but I was so tired. Besides, I needed to study for my exams. So I didn't go.

June 19, 1982

Rick and I broke up. *(This was the start of a pattern we repeated, and I eventually learned to regret, as I grew up to realize how naïve I was at that age. There were other guys worth my time.)*

July 30, 1982

As for Lancerettes, my best friend and I won't be in the routine for camp because, on the day of tryouts for it, I felt dizzy, as if I'd been on a carnival ride I usually avoid, so we left and didn't try out. Maybe I was hungry or something. It doesn't really bother us, though; we are still going to camp, which is next week!

November 25, 1982

I didn't realize how important it is to me for me to have Thanksgiving dinner with my family. My mom and Raul left this morning for Santa Domingo. It was a long, lonely Thanksgiving Day.

January 22, 1983

I sure wish I hadn't skipped writing about Christmas. It really was beautiful; just being with the family is enough for me.

July 22, 1983

I'm so glad to see summer finally arrive. So far this summer, I've gotten a job. I'm working at a title insurance company making copies, filing, running errands (my favorite,) and whatever else is necessary. Which brings me to the reason for me writing in my journal: I got a new car! I couldn't have done it without Raulito's help. He is my stepbrother (Raul, Jr.). The car is a stick shift. It's so much fun to drive (once he showed me how to drive it!). Well, I'm exhausted. I didn't sleep a wink last night. I was so excited about my new car!

Wednesday, September 28, 1983

It is 9:52 a.m. Just one more class to go! I can't wait to go home tonight and sleep! I want to go to Nautilus tonight if I can manage to get enough energy!

August 24, 1983

Today was the first day of school. It's my senior year. I love all four of my classes. I'm working 12:00 to 5:00 every day after school. I get out of school at 11:00 a.m. No Lancerettes this year. I chose not to try out. I'm ready to move on. It's time to think about my future. My junior year was fun, but I feel like I want to be finished with high school and start planning my future. That's why I attended summer school. I wanted to get one of my credits out of the way (History). I think I want to be a nurse. I haven't forgotten the Summer of '76, which I spent in and out of the hospital with a blood clot in my left calf that led to bleeding from my kidneys, that led to questions from all those involved in my care. You think, maybe, the blood thinner I was on might be causing the bleeding? That was then; now it's my chance to learn, for myself, what nursing really involves, if that's what I choose to do. Oh, I'm tired.

Saturday, December 17, 1983

Yesterday was the last day of school before Christmas break. I've had a headache, so I stayed home and rested today.

Friday, October 7, 1983, 8:50 a.m.

In about five minutes I'm about to ask my Trigonometry teacher for a recommendation to drop Trig class. I don't really want to drop any of my classes, but it's either that or lose my job, which is something I can't afford to do (as much as I'd like to). If I didn't have car payments, I'd quit my job in a minute. I really wish I didn't have to drop this class.

October 10, 1983

My Trig teacher won't give me a recommendation because I'm passing her class. I'm passing, but I can afford to drop it. I don't need it to graduate. I have very little time to study or do the necessary homework for this class. If I can't do my best, I don't want it to affect my GPA. Pass? I know I can do better! The guidance counselor said she would talk to her. (*I eventually ended up dropping this class.*)

Friday, October 21, 1983, 7:30 a.m.

It's Homecoming today! It's nothing like last year. To me, it seems like just another day. I won't even make it to our pep rally because I have to work. I hope I'll be able to see the parade while I'm on my runs. These are choices I made, though, and I'm really okay with them. You are in charge of your life determined by the choices you make. I feel as though I'm done with high school! I've gotten my scholarship. Next? I'm ready!

December 17, 1983

Yesterday was the last day of school before two weeks off for Christmas and New Year's. Last Tuesday, I stayed home from school because of a headache. The pain in my head makes it hard to concentrate on school work.

December 25, 1983

Last night we had our traditional dinner in our new house. My younger stepsister, Anita, came over with her son and daughter. Dinner was yummy as always. It was cold outside, the temperatures in the 30s. My feet were ice cold! I can only take so much of the cold weather.

March 24, 1984

Great news! I've been accepted into the Nursing Program at PBJC (Palm Beach Junior College)! There was a long waiting list for this program. Great start for my future! I plan to go there, and then continue my education at PBAC (Palm Beach Atlantic College). (*I would spend the next two years, including summer, to complete this program.*) I must take so many classes, and receive no lower than a "C," to keep my scholarship and graduate having completed this program. I can do this!

(*It turned out only four students were accepted directly from high school. I found this out as I graduated with 200 to 400 students in the Nursing Program.*)

Also, I applied for a job at Jordan Marsh. Vivian, my older stepsister, works there and has already given me a good recommendation, so I wasn't too nervous. I hope I get it! (*I did.*)

July 7, 1984

I graduated from John I. Leonard High School in June. I'm glad my senior year finally came to an end. I joined another fitness center. I feel much better now that I'm exercising.

Summer was over before I know it. My boyfriend went away to college. We eventually broke up.

Of course, attending college wasn't stressful enough! Hey, why don't I get married, too? I'm always with Allan anyway. He helps me study and is kind to me. I feel good with him. He supports me, always. He hates to see me cry. He tells me I can do it when I dare to doubt myself as I complete my nursing school. I often take my large nursing books to study while at the beach. He is a lifeguard, but I never paid attention to lifeguards. I had studying to do!

I was about nineteen years old when we got married. He was twenty-six. Once we got married, I would lie on the sand next to the lifeguard tower. One day, someone approached me and asked me, "When are you going to take off your cover up?

I heard Allan tell him, "Hey, leave her alone!"

The guy replied, "What's it to you?:

Allan said, with a serious look on his face, "That's my *wife!*"

That's when it hit me: I'm somebody's *wife!* Everything is happening so fast. What's my hurry? I would go to the beach on days he was working. As I read my big books, I noticed my vision was blurry. Mom took me to her ophthalmologist, who told me I was reading too much! He got me fitted for glasses to assist me with my reading. I would bring my glasses and books to the beach, where Allan thoughtfully set up an umbrella for me next to the lifeguard tower. Wasn't that sweet? I was getting way too much sun!

I am so young, and I have so much to learn about love, life, everything. (*And I will, the hard way.*) For now, I'm feeling invincible. I'm happy. I feel like nothing could get in my way. This *life* thing is *easy!*

2

TWENTY

May 22, 1986

I just turned twenty years old! It's been almost six months since Allan and I got married. I can't believe it. I just turned twenty years old! Allan is working the 3-to-11 p.m. shift as a medic on an ambulance. Our *plan* is, once I finish nursing school, he can attend college for respiratory therapy. He is still working as a lifeguard full time.

Did I say *plan?*

May 26, 1986

Today is Memorial Day. I went to the beach where Allan is working. I've been as careful as I can in the sun. I put on sunscreen and cover my face as well as possible. I have to protect my skin! Also, I've decided to get into the best shape imaginable. I'm trying to eat less and healthier. Currently, I'm five foot eight and I weigh 120 pounds. I'll end up being five-nine for the rest of my adult life thanks to genes, eating habits, and decisions I make to take care of the body I was given; that means no drugs and very little alcohol. I don't really care for that junk anyway. To me it's a cop-out. I have yet to find a substantial purpose for exposing myself to these items. If it were for stress relief, chances are the stress would still be there after the junk, only then I'd have more problems because I'd get to confront the stress *without* a clear head and, possibly, addiction, which means *more* stress!

This decision is all up to me.

I'm learning how *most* decisions are, actually, up to me.

July 17, 1986

State Board exams are finally over! It was tough, but now I can start working more and making good money. I've been working at St. Mary's Hospital as a GN (graduate nurse). I like working there, especially in the nursery.

July 26, 1986

Last night was the second time I worked the 11-to-7 night shift. I never took a break and hardly ever sat down. I'm beat! My legs hurt. It's as though all my body's blood is located solely in my lower extremities. I really want to prop my legs up above my heart!

October 23, 1986

I have to get used to Allan working 8 a.m. to midnight on days he works on the ambulance. I don't see him at all on Thursdays! Well, I guess that won't matter once I start my new job at Wellington Regional Medical Center! Finally, I'm getting a full time job, even though it's the 3-11 shift. I'll be making two dollars more an hour, though, so it's worth it.

I lost the diamond on my engagement/wedding ring—oops. I think I lost it at the beach. Allan wasn't too happy. Nobody said being married was easy! We'll eventually replace it.

December 26, 1987

I'm sitting here in our first new home, thinking of what to write. It is our first home. No more renting!

That's not what I wanted to write about, though. I have been diagnosed with multiple sclerosis. MS is a chronic, progressive neurological disease of the central nervous system, which includes the brain and spinal cord.

Okay, in English, think of the central nervous system as a phone line. For example, my brain wants to call my legs, to tell them to walk, but there has been a severe storm that's knocked out the phone lines to my legs, so they don't get the message or the message gets to them some other way—say by carrier pigeon. This, of course, will cause a person to have difficulty walking. The more often the same area is damaged, the more chances the difficulty will become permanent. There are different types of MS, and each person who has it is different from all the others, just as each person without MS is.

Those phone lines go everywhere in the body. I was diagnosed on November 18, 1987. I haven't worked since. I haven't gotten the nerve to write about it either until now. So much has happened. I was hospitalized for eight days at the hospital I had been working at overtime. I had been looking forward to the next day, my day off.

I recall the night I questioned how I felt the evening I asked about my symptoms. It was about 11 p.m. I was in my patient's room, which was dark. She was sound asleep (wish I'd been!). I couldn't get up from the side of her bed. I squatted down to read her output on the Foley catheter bag only to discover I had difficulty standing back up! Leaning on the edge of the bed, I struggle to get upright.

I made my way to the nurse's desk and asked if anyone knew of a neurologist there.

And there he was, looking like doctors are expected to, with his suit and tie, like a professional—Dr. Millan. Someone pointed him out to me.

I casually asked him, "What could be causing numbness and tingling on the left side of my body?" I wouldn't have asked *anyone*, but I'd had this symptom at that point for three days, and it was getting worse instead of better. That night, I was even tripping as I made my way through the hallway because I couldn't feel my left foot. My left hand had barely any sensation either, which made it tough to handle papers, pens, even folders doctors would ask me to hand to them.

The first possibility he mentioned was MS.

I thought, *No way!* and asked, "What, uh, what *else* could it be?" I was more willing to believe I'd had a stroke. After all, I *had* had a blood clot years before.

When he examined me in the staff lounge, he asked me if I was in charge. "Yes," I told him, wishing he would hurry. I had charting to do before giving a report to the next nurse. I could see there was something wrong with my left side, though. I couldn't even touch my nose with my left hand without difficulty.

Still, I refused to believe I had MS. I told myself it was "just nerves." After all, that's what I had been told when I was in high school; Dr. Berger had said it was "just nerves" and would go away, and it did.

The following day, though, Dr. Millan's office called me at home (on my day off, after working too many days with overtime) to tell me he'd scheduled me for an MRI.

I really need today *off*, I thought. But I dragged myself to my car and managed to get to St. Mary's. When the technician finished doing the MRI, he told me to go to Dr. Millan's office. Fine, I was thinking—by then, I was curious, confused, and wiped out. I just wanted to go home and *rest*. Nevertheless, I hauled myself back to our Mustang GT stick shift (that's work to drive in itself!).

I got to Millan's nearby office. As he was examining me, he got a call from the MRI Center to tell him I'd just left, and they gave him the results.

He hung up, looked at me with concern written all over his face, and told me the MRI had been positive for MS.

I sank my head into my hands, crying, feeling alone, thinking, This can't be *happening*. I asked myself, Why am I solo? "Don't," he said, gently resting his hand on my shoulder.

I looked up at him inquisitively.

"Crying will only make it worse," he said. How little is known about this illness. How I really needed someone to comfort me, to tell me they would be there for me. I just needed a *hug!* I assured myself, though, that someone, *anyone*, would be there for me, as I have always been there for others, right? Treat others the way you way you want to be treated?

I called Allan, who was home by then, and told him the news. "Can you come and pick me up?" But before he answered, I told him, "No, never mind. I'm coming home. I drove here, I can drive home."

As I got ready to go, Dr. Millan stopped me to tell me he was admitting me to WRMC, the hospital I'd just been working at for several days!

I assured him I could drive.

Allan was waiting for me on the patio, and I got my hug. It seemed as if it was too short (I think we were both in shock).

I went into the our villa to pack for the hospital. I was awfully scared by then. This was not supposed to be *happening*. It was not the *plan*.

They put me in the extra-large suite, which had a dining- room table, some other extras not found in other rooms, and a fold-out sleep sofa. Allan and I slept there every night. He comforted me by telling me he wasn't going anywhere. I didn't doubt him. I knew I could count on him.

During my stay, I was visited by several co-workers and doctors I'd worked with as a nurse. Only I was suddenly a patient, and they were acquaintances or friends.

I will remember one doctor in particular for what he told me. He kindly said, *"You're still Alys. I see you doing something with this diagnosis. You won't let it change who you are. You're going to do something about it."*

I eventually joined the local chapter of the MS Society board until it closed in this area. I respected him, having worked with him, because I had observed his behavior towards his patients. Many nurses would complain about taking orders from him. But he was specific, thorough, and confident about care for his patients. Some nurses saw the work he created for us as a bother;

I admired his patient care. I would tell those nurses, "If I ever need an infectious-disease specialist, he's my guy!" (He did in fact become my physician for a brief time before he moved away—my loss.)

While I was there, I also switched to another neurologist, one I remembered treating a patient with MS.

But now I'm with Dr. Millan again. Since they discharged from the hospital the day before Thanksgiving, I have gone from bad to worse. I had terrible vertigo and shortness of breath with even the slightest exertion, as though an elephant was sitting on my chest. I was nauseated. I felt like crap. When I expressed my complaints to this other neurologist, he said my examination had showed I had recovered a hundred percent from the exacerbation, and nothing was wrong with me.

I thought, In that case, I'm losing my mind! and said to him, "How can you say nothing is *wrong* with me? My left leg is weak, I walk like a klutz, and I feel *awful!*"

I didn't sleep at all that night. The next day, I called Millan and told him how I felt. The day after that, I was in his office, and he's been taking care of me ever since. I had been wrong to change doctors. From the moment Millan examined me that night in the staff lounge, he'd kept up with me, ordering the MRI, having his office call me the next day—he'd even brought the MRI films to my hospital room to show me the results. He owed me nothing. I should have listened to my gut feeling: Trust yourself, nobody knows you better than you. But I had been in shock.

How do I feel today? Well, I'm taking Antivert for the vertigo; I was walking better over a week ago than I am today. One day, I felt so good, I was nonstop for the entire day (cleaning the house, shopping, I even went to Lily's house—she's Raul's sister, who is also a seamstress) to get my dress altered for the WRMC Christmas party. I'm wiped out now. That night, I had excruciating pain in my left thigh. After a week, the pain progressed to my entire left leg and right leg. Anaprox and naprosyn did nothing for the pain. So here I sit with pain in my legs, dragging my left leg when I walk. Now, the numbness is back in my left thigh. I really screwed up that day I went gallivanting around. This is the price I pay. My leave of absence is up on the thirtieth of the month. I can barely walk. I use a cane.

The party was great, by the way. I even won a prize, and I never win *anything!*

I don't know how to describe how I felt when I limped slowly to the front of the room, with my cane, to get my prize, and everyone applauded. I needed that. Allan helped me get back to my seat.

Almost forgot—I'm seeing Dr. Bortnick (a psychologist) for relaxation techniques. I've had an awful time sleeping. It's important I get adequate rest with this disease. Since I've been seeing him, I'm sleeping better at night but I still feel as if I could sleep another eight hours. I still get depressed sometimes when I'm alone. I think about this disease and how unpredictable it is, and, worse, that there is no cure. It's hard for me to "relax" when I want to live each day to the fullest. I'm so young. I have too many things to do. It's hard to just relax. I hate MS.

December 27, 1987

I never have nightmares. Since I was discharged from the hospital, I've had five I can remember:

1. I'm lying in the grass. It's a beautiful day. The trees are tall. The leaves are green. I have my right arm stretched up next to my right ear. There is a friendly brown dog lying on my right arm. His fur is fluffy on my skin. I want to move my right arm. As soon as I attempt to, though, the dog becomes a mean, black creature with sharp, pointed teeth, and he growls angrily. His face is only inches from mine. I say to my husband, "Allan, is there a dog on me?" This is when I realized it was only a bad dream. I couldn't believe I had woken up my husband to ask him if a dog was on me!

2. I'm having an affair with someone at work. My husband is having an affair with someone I know. I had this dream the night before our second anniversary. It was so real! I spent most of the following day convinc-

ing myself it was only a dream. Who wants to be alone at such a time in their life? I woke up with a terrible headache on the entire left side of my head. I couldn't even open my left eye. I've had a headache one other time since then.

3. I'm in a hospital bed, sleeping. All of a sudden my left arm starts moving wildly, and I can't control it. I can't even *feel* it. I just stare with fright as I see my arm moving. Then I scream and yell for my mother to "Stop my arm!" I'm crying and yelling. What a nightmare. A few days before this dream I'd had an Evoke Potential. During this diagnostic test, impulses passing through my left hand had caused my hand to move, sort of like tremors, without my control. Painless, but what a bad feeling I had getting it done. Allan was at work. Raul dropped me off. I was alone. It was like a bad dream.

4. Allan is cheating on me again. I must have been feeling isolated, on my own with this disease. God, I hate those dreams.

5. Last night, I dreamt I was in the hospital with MS and couldn't pee. This is the same symptom I remember the patient with MS was admitted with. That's probably why I dreamt about it. It's the first symptom that comes to mind when I think of MS. How can this basic function of the human body become problematic? In my dream, a Foley catheter was inserted to relieve the

situation. The urine was thick and brown, not like typical bright-yellow urine. I say, "I must have UTI!" That is one of the worst MS complications.

January 5, 1988

New Year's Eve. Allan has to work tomorrow so he went to sleep at 11:00 p.m. I stayed up to watch Dick Clark and called my sister, who was also spending the Eve alone. I woke up Allan at midnight (he wasn't too happy). Anyway, the next day was better. We opened a bottle of champagne and watched a movie on our new VCR.

Since I'm sleeping better, I am no longer seeing Dr. Bortnick. I made a copy of the relaxation tapes he sent me.

I still have pain in both my legs. It feels like marbles are lodged beneath my skin, with various pressure points. Three days ago, I started feeling pain and burning in my arms. The doctor I was referred to for rehab said the only rehab he would prescribe right now is what I'm already doing. Exercise would only aggravate the pain because it originates in the central nervous system. I'm just supposed to relax and take a nap during the day. I could have given myself that prescription and conserved the energy I used to get dressed, get in my car, get out of my car, wait, wait, wait in his waiting room, then drive my fatigued, painful, frustrated self home! My left thigh is numb and weaker than before. It collapses when I attempt to use it.

My leave of absence is up, as I have already mentioned

on December 30. But I am told by these doctors, "No work for at least another month. They will, of course, *not* pay my bills. I'm just kidding. That was *funny?* Really, I want to *work!* Besides, I don't expect others to pay my bills or solve my problems. They're all mine. I don't have to share them with anybody, kind of like this disease. Others can just walk away. MS is still here, occasionally reminding me of its presence, with a dig here and there known as a "symptom" to others, but as *hell* to *me.* So I cry. Wasn't that helpful? I ask myself when I'm done crying. Now what? I've just used my limited energy to cry, thinking, *Poor me,* and I didn't accomplish anything! I have just *wasted my valuable energy.* And that's the take-away, the lesson I must learn: *Negative energy is wasted energy.* So here I sit with less energy.

The other night, Allan and I went to Palm Beach and sat on a bench, watching airplanes come in over the ocean towards PBIA. It was a beautiful night. The moon was full, the weather perfect—perfect therapy, just what *this* doctor (I myself) ordered. The other therapy helpful to me is when Allan plays his acoustic guitar and sings the Beatles' "Dear Prudence" but replace "Prudence" with "Alys." See? My therapy is free—and effective!

January 7, 1988

Yesterday morning I woke up with terrible pain and burning in both my arms. I mistakenly thought the bed was on fire! It woke me up several times that night. I also began to feel the same discomfort throughout my back. I reported these symptoms, which also included weakness, to Dr. Millan. He started me back on steroids for two weeks. He also prescribed Pamelor for the pain. Well, it hasn't relieved the pain yet. I hurt more today than I did yesterday (if that's possible). I can't believe how much.

I went to a specialist to confirm that my vertigo was not being caused by some condition other than MS. I was told the labarcynthitis had possibly been triggered by MS (*No kidding, I thought—so why am I seeing you again? I know proof is needed for diagnosis but what will it change?*).

January 21, 1988

I can't believe how bad the pain in my legs is today. Increasing the Pamelor for pain hasn't caused any noticeable improvement. I'm scheduled for an electronystagmogram to determine if my vertigo is related a problem with my inner ear. To be MS-related, it should show up on my MRI, but no lesions appear in that area. (I haven't had this until now. I know they need to see it, but I don't know how it would really change anything.)

We got our spa hooked up! It feels so good to sit in it. I have to make sure it's not too hot for me, though, so it doesn't aggravate my symptoms.

I'm having difficulty staying on my feet without unbearable pain. I'm going for an interview today for a weight-loss clinic. It only pays eight dollars an hour, but I've always wanted to do something like this because it's different. Now seems like the best time. Any money I can make is better than staying home and doing nothing. The only problem is, I don't know if I should tell them I have MS. I don't know if they would hire me. I'm not so sure *I* would hire me! I hope I can walk into the office without a cane and not look like I'm drunk! I feel so uncoordinated without support from a cane or anything else I can hold on to. Well, I'll just walk slowly and carefully, and pray I do well.

I can't believe I still have this vertigo! It's been two months and two days (not that I'm keeping track—ha). Last week I got extremely dizzy and nauseated, as if I'd had a terrible ride at the fair. This feeling appeared yesterday as well.

I wish the pain in my entire body would just *disappear.* Dr. Millan says I will have it for a long time. (I will, but I will also eventually learn how much more challenging other symptoms can be—and how strong I really am.)

Tuesday, January 26, 1988

I got a job! Starting Monday, I will be an admitting nurse at WRMC. I'm so happy! I'm so grateful to my employer for allowing me to continue with the same pay and benefits as I had upstairs! How fortunate for me. I still am unaware of how grateful I should be for having been given this opportunity. I have no idea that I could just as easily have been encouraged to leave this hospital and find other work. Thank you, WRMC!

I still have vertigo, though. Yesterday, I had an EGD done. If results show it is normal, that means the vertigo is more than likely from the MS (duh).

I still have pain. The aching isn't as bad, but the burning is equally as uncomfortable as in the past. The other day it felt like severe sunburn. My left thigh still feels numb and weak. I notice it most at the end of the day.

March 6, 1988

I'm so *tired*. I haven't had a good night's sleep in days. I was feeling good for a couple of days, so, I think, I took advantage of that and bypassed my allotted level of energy! Now I'm back with the pain. It's everywhere. It feels like a serious case of the flu! I feel miserable and I just hate it! My vertigo has in fact improved but occasionally makes an unwelcome appearance. I have brief bouts of horrible pain. I might as well be giving birth without anesthesia!

I was prevented from returning to work for an additional couple of weeks because a co-worker had the chicken pox, and I had zero titer. I've never had the chicken pox or most of any of the childhood illnesses that I can remember.

Allan and I are growing further and further apart. Having to adjust to this uninvited guest, MS has been difficult for both of us—not part of our vision for our future, not what we expected. Expectations lead to disappointment.

Wednesday, May 25, 1988

Hating this disease, I'm working Monday, Wednesday, and Friday from noon to 6:00 p.m. My arms and legs experience excruciating pain at the end of each day.

Allan's father invited us on a seven-day cruise—his treat during our birthday! Allan is seven years older. Our birthdays are days apart. It's probably not a great idea to get on a boat when you have vertigo! But I want to go! I want Allan to be with me if I don't go. I feel so out of control of my decisions right now, as though the MS is in control of my choices, not *me*. He ends up taking the cruise with his family *without me*. I'm hurt but not surprised. I know he needs a break from the presence of this disease. Where's *my* break? I cry, alone, again.

My life is kind of screwed up right now. Allan and I are talking about a separation. This will eventually lead to divorce. It is a difficult time in my unpredictable life. But everything happens for a reason, I guess. I'm desperately searching for an explanation of what I'm going through.

November 1, 1988

Our divorce is almost final.

As far as work is concerned, I quit the admitting office, now I'm back upstairs on 2W (my original position, but now I'm per-diam and doing four-hour shifts at J.F.K. Hospital. The money is great. I kind of overdid it last week, my first week back upstairs at WRMC. So, this week, my body is getting me back. I have pain in both my legs and weakness in my right one. I'm back on steroids for two weeks and out of work for this one. I just can't get a break. I'm distraught, overwhelmed, and feeling that nobody understands, or wants to for that matter. Let me just cry for just a tiny bit. . .okay, I'm done. Sometimes I just need to.

No, what I need is a plan for when I feel this way.

November 6, 1988

It's done. The divorce was finalized last week. Finalized, but I still feel as if Allan is there to listen to me if no one else will. Funny thing about divorce—we actually get along better! Let me just mention, again, how *young* I am!

3

IT

November 20, 1988

It's been one year since my diagnosis.

I miss when Allan played with my hair when we went to bed. It would put me right to sleep.

November 25, 1988

Today was a great day! I felt good, *fantastic*. The first thing I did *when* I woke up was write a poem. It's called "MS and Me." I'm not a poet, I just find writing a poem at certain times is therapeutic for me.

December 1, 1988

It's supposed to get into the fifties tonight! That's a nice change from this hot Florida weather.

I've been dating a guy, Derrick. He's kind to me. I'm lonely. I feel beautiful around him.

He eventually ends up moving in with me, helps with the bills. I got a dog! He is a Shih-tzu. He's black and white, adorable.

Zubi, my Shi-tsu, was a perfect companion and always happy to see me.

I feel fantastic. The best I've felt since I was diagnosed. I barely have any pain! *Yeah!*

January 3, 1989

I can't believe its 1989! New Year's Eve was fun. Derrick and I spent the evening at Timmy's house. He is my younger of two step-sisters' boyfriend, who had a small party. On New Year's Day, we celebrated the night by going dancing at a local club with them and another couple. We had a great time. I'm feeling like a *normal twenty-three-year-old—partying, dating a hot, tall, sexy, man who can't keep his eyes or hands off me. I feel pretty. I needed that. MS is not so pretty. I'm going to remember this feeling whenever the MS makes its appearance, so I can show this positive attitude to others and give myself a dose of self-esteem. People see you as you see yourself.*

Christmas Eve went well also. The whole family (sister and step-siblings) were at my parents' house. The previous night, Anita, Raulito, and I went to another club to dance. We had a great time. Derrick didn't want to go. He doesn't care much for dancing.

He changed his mind about that quickly, though! We ended up going to clubs frequently. He tells me he enjoys watching me dance. I enjoy the feeling he gives me by complimenting me!

January 17, 1989

I have worked one day so far this year. Today is Tuesday. On Sunday, I worked three hours at Wellington Regional and four at John F. Kennedy Hospital. I took nine patients there! When I got home, my legs hurt so badly. The worst symptom was the fatigue. I was so wiped out that I almost couldn't take a shower. I cried all night. I was so upset, realizing my body can't handle taking a patient assignment. That's just another reminder that I still have MS.

Derrick has been really good to me, telling me he loves me and is there for me. *I'm* sure MS is prepared to challenge those words. He's gotten a job close to home that pays well.

Well, I joined Tri-county Home Health Care last week. The DON (Director of Nursing) used to work at WRMC. I trust her to give me assignments I can tolerate!

February 18, 1989

Today was not a good day. The pain in my left side has gotten worse. It started five days ago with a "hot" feeling of my left arm, especially when I would touch a "cold" object. Bizarre, isn't it? By Friday it involved my entire left side down to my foot, except my neck and face. Dr. Millan is out of town until Monday. I will see him then. I just got over a bad cold/flu.

I've been working steadily for Tri-county Home Health Care doing IV therapy and A.M. care for a quadriplegic man twenty-seven years old. He is of average build, a good-looking Caucasian who just had *his* entire life plan completely change from what he had planned. He was on a motorcycle, getting a ride from a friend after a party they attended. He tells me he was close to home. I tell him how unexpected life can be with a caring look on my face. I can't let them know I have MS because a nurse with polio was there and they asked her not to come back.

I saw this patient frequently and become close to him and his family, eventually informing them of my diagnosis. They kindly welcomed me to their home. Heck, I think I took him to the beach to get him out of the house! It was walking distance from their home.

Thursday, February 23, 1989

Well, I have been a patient at WRMC for three days now. My dad has yet to call me. I'm not surprised. I'm hurt. I need my daddy. I don't know what is presently going on in his life; I'm a *little* preoccupied with what is going on in mine. He does eventually call me. I don't really feel much different since I got here. My left side still hurts, especially when touched by any object, person, or just me! My handwriting is sloppy because I now have weakness in my right side. I feel as if I'm cut in half! My left side burns as if on fire. It gets worse when touched by cold hands or objects, as though I've stuck my left side into a campfire. I'm clumsy when I walk. Dr. Millan is ordering ACTH intravenous for me. This is the first time I've had this to treat MS. My mom has been there for me, always. She is an awesome example for me if I ever become a mom. Getting a different treatment concerns me. I need to be optimistic, though.

I can't believe how hard it has been to get an IV started on me. My veins just disappear!

February 25, 1989

Yesterday was my first day of physical therapy. I felt better before exercise. I experienced elevated levels of pain of my left leg. I was given a shot to alleviate the pain, but I think the nurse gave me *more* medicine than ordered! I couldn't see straight or keep my eyes open for lunch. I was zonked for two and a half hours!

I feel better today. My left arm is improving; I can feel more with my fingers. The back of my arm is still numb, though. My entire left side is numb too, as well as painful. The weakness continues to trouble me when I use my left thigh. So I have the sensation of iced areas with the strength of an infant, and areas of pain similar to that experienced by people in torture chambers. Jcy. I just want to go home.

Monday, March 6, 1989

My handwriting is back to normal (*yippee!*).

God gave this disease to the wrong person. He should have given it to someone stronger than me, someone more prepared, someone with a stable marriage and sufficient funds, someone with better coping skills. I don't know how much more I can take. I just wish it would go away. I can't handle the pain. I can't handle the way it's affecting my life. I try so hard. I don't know what to do. I want to be able to take care of *myself*. I want to pay *my* bills. I want to be in *control*. I'm not the kind of person who is easily *dependent* on another. It's driving me crazy. I feel so helpless, useless.

All the money I put into my home. . .and it doesn't even feel like home. It's a house. I can't live like this anymore. I've had MS over a year and three months now, and it's just beginning to sink in. Every time I have pain, I am reminded how my nervous system is not normal, sending messages incorrectly because of plaques, scarred areas in my brain and spinal cord. God, it's really there. I can't even take a shower without pain. It feels like I'm being attacked by marbles continuously being thrown at me, especially on my left side.

I'm unable to clean my own house. I can't get a job, a steady one, anyway. I'm sure Derrick is sick of paying the bills. I'm sick of depending on him TO pay them! I don't know what to do. I think the MS is winning this fight. I called it. I said MS would challenge the relationship between Derrick and me. Why bother getting close to someone? He doesn't have to stay. He doesn't have to deal with any of this disease. He can easily just walk away. I need a friend.

I don't think I have learned the true meaning of love. If this is love, then why do I feel so very lonely? I guess what I'm trying to say is that maybe there is no such thing as Mr. Perfect.

I just need to get my priorities straight. One thing I know for sure is that I need to make some money, so I will be prepared for when I am alone. Allan tells me he loves me and would live here again and take care of my problems. *What?* I don't think so. It was so hard to get separated from him. I can't do it again. I don't know if he really loves me. I don't really know what I want. I'm just writing gibberish. I know I'm not happy. So many people are worse off than me. Knowing that doesn't make me feel any better. I feel I'm going to explode. I have so much to say, and no one to listen.

Sometimes I tell Allan if I'm hurt or depressed. He cheers me up. I have no regrets about our divorce. I pursued it following my diagnosis. I guess I was thinking, This is my battle, not his. It's that *control* thing again. Depression is anger turned inward. That makes sense. I'm so angry I could cry.

I finally worked today for Tri-county Homecare. I did a case in Jupiter. I still have pain in my left torso and left arm. I am unable to tell temp with my left fingers. The pain is severe when I'm touched, especially with something cold. It feels like electric current-high voltage. I hate it. I hate this medicine, Tegretol. I quit Sinequan two days ago, so I'm sleeping poorly. I took Halcyon tonight, so I should sleep well. I need to.

Saturday, November 11, 1989

I can't believe how quickly this year has gone by! It hasn't been easy. I had period of time when I was feeling well. I even had a full-time job. That lasted all of four to six weeks. It seems things go from bad to worse nowadays. I was doing contract work for two home-care agencies when my upper lip and toes on my left foot got numb.

I was admitted to JFK hospital for ACTH (adrenocorticotropic hormone) treatment. I was there from October 5 to 11. I made some friends, plus a lot of co-workers I knew from Wellington were there.

While there, I had difficulty breathing. What next! I also had weakness of my left thigh. I went home with a low-grade temperature, which I'd had throughout my hospital stay. The second night at home, I had a terrible cough and a sore throat. Wonderful, just what I needed. errick was giving me ACTH injections per orders from Dr. Millan because my condition was not improving. I was getting worse. The pain and weakness in my left leg were pretty bad. I still have physical therapy at home, and my whole body shakes with tremors when I exercise.

On Tuesday, Mom, Derrick, and I went to The University of Miami to see an MS specialist, Dr. Sheremata. Dr. Millan had said there was nothing more he could do for me, so he had referred me to him.

I made my way to his office, smiling, with my long dark brown hair and fit body. I feel good right now. Dr. Sheremata was very helpful about answering my questions. He can't treat me until he knows what kind of MS I have (mild, exacerbation remission, or progressive). So he had my blood drawn for HLA DR, and those results will help determine my care. Unfortunately, they won't be in for two weeks.

They are the longest two weeks of my life. I feel I'm just getting worse. The pain in my legs is disabling, plus my legs are weak and my left leg is getting number. If that's not enough, my fatigue is more apparent than ever. I do practically nothing all day. What's worse is that, when I walk, I can't tell where my legs are, so I have to walk slowly. I look like a drunk. What a change from when I saw Dr. Sheremata. I was feeling good, normal, that day. The unpredictability of this disease makes planning anything in my life practically impossible. Still, I continue to do so. I have to. I hate this disease. But I will keep the positive attitude that has worked well for me in the past.

I am now receiving food stamps, kind of humiliating but it's not *my fault*. I can't work. I have to keep reminding myself of this. Derrick is financially unpredictable. I must be able to take care of myself.

March 21, 1990

I know now I am stronger than I thought I was. I know I just have to have faith and believe God will help me.

When I went to the MS Update seminar in Fort Lauderdale, I met many people with MS and family members of those with MS as well. I got there walking, but it was a long walk, so Derrick carried me piggy back as he often does without giving it a second thought. It's normal to me, but from the look of others staring at us, maybe not so normal to them. Hey, when we went to Sunfest or the Greek Festival, we did the same thing. People would stare or comment about how they wanted a ride, too! No big deal. I love him for allowing me to skip the wheelchair!

Anyway, what really surprised me was how everyone seemed amazed about my attitude toward this MS disease. Then I looked around and saw how those there with MS appeared so sad and hopeless. My God, how do they make it through each day with that attitude? I thought *I* wasn't handling it well! *I'm not alone.*

I'm going to talk to those people when it's possible. I hope I can show them how having a positive attitude greatly impacts the course of this diagnosis. If I can give even one person purpose for their presence in this thing we call life, they, in turn, will make my life worth living. I keep reminding myself, *I am not alone!*

4

IDIOT

May 25, 1990

Wow! So much has happened since the last time I wrote, in March. I was in the hospital again in February at WRMC. I had an attack when Derrick moved out. It was a mutual decision. He even helped me find a roommate. He and I continue to date, but we also date others, kind of. I put an ad in the newspaper and was fortunate to get a decent male roomie. Hopefully, I'll get my bills paid in a timely manner! That's me, sick but responsible!

I made a very special friend, Scott. I met his parents at the MS seminar in March. They attended the seminar because Scott has MS. Apparently, he's been having quite a time dealing with this diagnosis. They wanted me to call him, which I did. We agreed to meet, so I drove my Mazda RX7 to his home, a condo in Fort Lauderdale along

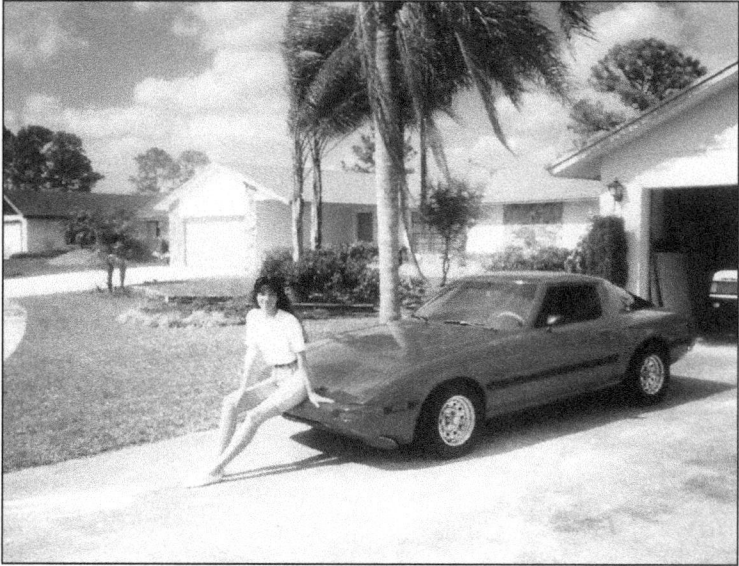

With my cherry-red Mazda RX-7

the Intracoastal Waterway. I was having a good day as far as the MS was concerned. I had been looking forward to meeting him, this kind voice I'd been speaking to often on the phone. We'd exchanged our stories about how we were living with this horrid disease. He'd often say, "This disease sucks!" I'd giggle in agreement.

I was finally getting the chance to put a face to the voice. I felt I already knew him. We share many things in common besides MS. Aside from our birthdays being in May, we enjoy similar interests, and our ages are close enough to share commonalities!

When I met him, I was pleasantly surprised. He is of average height with brown hair parted to the side and deep blue eyes, and he uses a cane to ambulate. It felt as if I was seeing an old friend who'd been away for too long. We instantly greeted each other and exchanged smiles, handshakes, and hugs. I was so *comfortable* in his presence. I could see us spending a lot of time together. I hoped I could give him at least a little comfort in knowing that I have the same fears and frustrations that he does. He had already given that to me.

So Scott and I ended up spending lots of time together. We've do many things like going out for lunch at T.G.I. Friday's. He hadn't been there in two years! He'd made the mistake of letting MS control *him* instead of controlling his decisions *despite* the disease. He even parked in the handicapped space, upon my insistence! I told him, "It's a long walk to the door, so use my permit if you don't have one." I forget whether he had it; I believe he did. Regardless, parking there was difficult for him. But I went on, "Who cares if we park here? Just because we don't fit the expected profile of handicapped doesn't mean we're doing something illegal! If other people choose to judge us, that's their problem. I have trouble walking long distances, so I need to park *here*."

After careful consideration, he did. It was no big deal. We had a fantastic time and have repeated that journey many times!

We enjoy doing many things together, even if it's just staying at his home playing board games, watching

T.V., or talking. He taught me how to play chess. No wonder I didn't care for it, I didn't know how to play it! Love it now! It's one of the games we enjoy playing. We often hate what we don't understand.

His condo is *cold!* Scott has a blanket ready for me because it feels like a refrigerator when I walk in. He doesn't tolerate heat well.

I will never forget one time we went out in my car. When we got back to his home, I got out (I had driven). He got out, promptly fell onto the hot pavement, and couldn't get off the ground! I rushed to his side to help him, but, appearing somewhat embarrassed, he told me not to.

I told him with a smile on my face, "Don't be silly. Of *course* I'm going to help you."

After getting very little help from the security guard (liability issues, I guess), I thought, We need a wheelchair but have none. I said to Scott, "We need *wheels!* What about your office chair?" I ran into his condo and got it. With assistance of the guard, who was probably too embarrassed by then not to help, we propped Scott in the chair, and I rushed him inside.

Ahhhh, air conditioning: It perked him right up. The color returned to normal in his cheeks. I could see the relief in his face, not to mention the way his body had reacted to the cool conditions. Sitting up was much easier!

I'm currently helping him redecorate his condo. He knows I enjoy interior decorating. His home is already beautiful, but he's letting me redecorate anyway. We had fun going to the furniture store. We would sit on different sofas and look at various swatches to choose the decor.

Wait a minute, he's allowing me to decorate his home? I get the sense he just enjoys making me happy. He actually is pleased when I enjoy doing something that is fun for me. I am so lucky to be with someone who brings out the best in me. I feel good about myself when we are together. I love the way I look through his eyes.

Scott has been really good to me. He lets me help him with work on the computer at his home even though I have difficulty typing with the decreased sensation in my fingers. He could do it quicker, but he patiently allows me to earn money I refuse from him anyway. He knows I'm having trouble paying my bills. He works full time as an office manager. Each time I came over, he'd purposely slip a few dollars into my purse, or pocket, or however he could make sure he I had a few bucks for the gas I'd used to get to his home about forty-five minutes from mine. He'd tell me how he would follow me to my car if I refused. Knowing that I wouldn't want him to hurt himself battling the heat, I settled for whatever he wanted.

For his birthday, I wrote him a poem. I feel safe with him, meaning I can let my guard down when I am with him. He won't critique my poem; he will appreciate the thought I put into writing it. I believe I also gave him a gift, but I forget what it was—that's how important material gifts are. I believe I made him a flower arrangement for his coffee table to match the colors of his living room. I think he liked it. If not, he wouldn't tell me. He has more class then that. Well, he gave me a very special, meaningful gift for *my* birthday. I'm sure it cost him a pretty penny, but he says he wanted to get it for me.

After repeatedly opening boxes, starting with a very large box, and then another, slightly smaller one, I finally reached a very small box. Upon opening it, I saw a beautiful bracelet made letter "A"s (the first letter of my name) in gold, with the exception of one "A" made entirely of diamonds!

"I can't accept such a generous gift!" I told him as his family watched me open it. He said he wanted to get it for me and refused to take it back. He also sent a dozen roses to my home on by birthday. He gave me a real nice card, too. I think he really cares about me.

Derrick wants to marry me. I don't see this happening. When he moved out, it was because he didn't want to deal with paying the bills and credit cards he'd helped me ring up. So he moved out and left it all for me—an unemployed twenty-three-year-old with MS. I can just imagine what marriage to him would be like. It's so easy to say, "Marry me!" or "I love you." It's even easier to believe those words when my life is so difficult. I need a friend. Anyway, I just have to believe that everything will work out and God will show me what to do.

I'm an idiot. I haven't learned how I should be treated. I feel so out of control. I'm just along for the ride, taking whatever life throws at me. I haven't been taught how to manage my life properly. It's so *challenging!*

Monday, June 11, 1990

I just got over an attack of optic neuritis. I was seeing double (vertically). It was so frustrating because it was like watching T.V. out of focus. I thought I would never see straight again. I went to Dr. Bentz (an ophthalmologist). He said it should go away, and it did. He had seen me at WRMC in February, when the left side of my face was numb and my vision was blurry at times.

Anyway, Derrick and I have been getting along great. He repainted my RX7 a real nice red. I love it! My car looks brand new. He's been nice to me lately, but we got into an argument about my roommate's friend, whom I dated. As Scott says, I'm too nice. I know why I continue to see Derrick. I feel pretty and confident with him, even though we sort of broke up. I still haven't learned how I should be treated, even though it's smack in my face with Scott's treatment of me.

I've been doing so well lately. I'm still poor, but I feel so good that not having money seems so minor right now. It really scared me when I had double vision last week, though.

Scott called me tonight. I don't appreciate him calling Derrick *asshole* or *stupid*. He keeps telling me, "I know, when Derrick moves to West Palm next month, I won't see you anymore." He acts like he's my boyfriend or something. Did I mention I'm an idiot?

My friend just called. I went to high school with him. He's a nice guy. He's a chemist for a citrus company. He said he'd had a crush on me in high school! He told me he is living currently in Lakeland. I don't think he would hurt me because he seems to care quite a bit about me. He is kind and polite to me. At this point in my life, I'm searching for that friend I keep mentioning.

Thursday, June 21, 1990

It's the first day of summer! My friend from Lakeland just called. He's in town again, so we have plans to go out on Saturday. Derrick and I are getting along okay. He wasn't too thrilled to hear about my Saturday plans, but it's not his decision, is it? Allan calls occasionally as well, but Scott has figured me out. He tells me guys only get one chance with me. He knows me better than I know myself. He calls sometimes as well. Our relationship is somewhat comical in a serious way.

He remains my friend while I date these guys. I am permitted to call him at any time to describe my encounters with these guys, as well as how I feel when I'm out with them. Heck, I can call him any time, and I know he will listen to me cry and comfort me, always. He doesn't have to.

Saturday night was festive at best. My Lakeland friend and I had a great evening. We enjoy spending time together. We remain just friends, though. He is the kind of guy you marry. He keeps inviting me to visit him in Lakeland for a *little* vacation. (I never did, but Lord knows I should have! It would have been good for me, and I trust him.)

Upon my insistence, my mom and I went with Scott and his mother to see Dr. Sheremata for his first time. Currently, he is seeing a neurologist locally. I told him about how my local doctor had recommended I go to U of Miami to see Sheremata, since he is providing a range of treatments for MS. Up to now, Scott has been treated with Prednisone.

The journey to Miami seemed long, but our moms got along great and we tolerated the trip well. I think we all just liked having someone to voice our concerns over this illness. Valuable, we are not alone.

July 2, 1990

Scott hasn't been calling much. I hesitate to call him. I made a new friend, Gary. He has MS, too. I met him through Dr. Sheremata's office. I was talking to his nurse about participating in the Alpha Interferon Study. There have been some pretty good results so far. Anyway, she gave me Gary's phone number, because he is currently participating in this study.

Gary is so funny! He's great. He has a positive attitude, like me. He is in a wheelchair now, but he is working part time at an office where he does P.R. He is able to ambulate with crutches. Before taking interferon, he couldn't even get into a wheelchair by himself. I haven't met him yet. We've just talked on the phone.

My maternal grandmother is coming from Cuba! She will stay with me. She arrives July 16. She is coming for a visit because she wants to take care of me. Like many people with MS, though, I prefer taking care of myself.

I'm sure her visit will benefit my mom's separation from Raul, whom she continues to see and assist with his chronic obstructive pulmonary disease. He has quite a bit of trouble breathing (the result of smoking for years). In my eyes, separating from my mother is his attempt at controlling what he can. With the COPD, He is having much difficulty breathing.

July 9, 1990

I met Gary on Thursday—drove to his condo. He's fit, slim, and cute, too! He prepared a letter for me to send to my insurance company regarding paying for me to take interferon. Hopefully, I will. This medication is expensive. All I need is money!

Anyway, he is a really nice guy with lots of friends, as evidenced by activities he does with them and the plans he makes. His attitude towards MS is excellent. He is so positive! He made dinner for us from his wheelchair. I didn't dare help him. (I offered once, but he refused.) I know the satisfaction he gets from being independent.

He went to a concert with some of his friends later that night, so we didn't have as much time as I had hoped to talk. I'll probably see him this weekend. I'm still spending time with Derrick. Why? I don't know. I *do* know that I'm single and making decisions that don't affect anyone but me. It's kind of liberating.

My eye pain has lessened for now. I've been so fatigued. I worked Saturday. I saw four patients, but it drained me so much, I came home and lay on my bed for an hour because my body was so fatigued.

Wednesday, July 11, 1990

I worked today. I saw three patients. I figured that would be better than four because I could maybe get done earlier, before it got too hot outside. I finished at 11:00 a.m. It was so hot anyway. God, that fatigues me so much. I felt as if someone had sucked the life out of my body. I've got to make seven hundred dollars this month in order to pay my bills. The money I make per patient is good. Many nurses doing the same homecare rush through each visit in order to make more money. I know I could do the same (I *need* the money), but I do my complete assessment, answer questions about meds, teach if necessary. Isn't that what I'm paid for? That's how *I* would want to be treated. Okay, I know I could be quicker if necessary, but I enjoy speaking to these patients, and getting to know them as people rather than patients. I believe being a nurse as well as a patient at times has made me more empathetic towards these patients.

I'm sick of being poor, but I thank God I've made it this long. I'm glad Derrick is still being kind to me.

My mom loves her new job. She's working in bookkeeping for the school district. I'm glad to see her happy. It pleases me to see her doing well following the separation from my stepfather. She is showing me how to survive difficult times. I don't think this was part of her life plan! She's excited about seeing her mom. Just five more days!

My dog is so cute. He is just snoring away, lying in front of me on my bed. God, I love him. He keeps me company. My roommate is here tonight, so I am not alone. My legs hurt terribly all day. They are on fire. I think it's the heat, and that I'm doing too much. I've got to relax. I took Sinequan to help me sleep.

July 19, 1990

Abuela Olga is here! She is going to be staying in the middle room. I didn't go to Miami International Airport with my mom. My sister and her daughter Hanna went instead. *Abuela* came in at 2:00 a.m. They got to Mom's house at 6:00 a.m. It would have been difficult for me to have stayed up all night. Anyway, she came to my home Tuesday morning, and we went to the grocery store. She pushed me in my wheelchair. I think it helped her to confirm her visit, and I figured I could use the break from walking in the store. She probably felt needed. Nildy, Hanna, and I took her to the store to buy shoes (she arrived in America wearing borrowed shoes to go with the beautiful dress she was wearing, which was made from a bedspread!

Her stay has been enlightening. To hear about her life in a country with many limitations but very little food, I am amazed at her behavior towards *her* life. How does she do it? She tells funny stories about her everyday struggle. She occasionally smiles when telling us of the struggles she encounters on a daily basis. She talks about going up and down stairs, waiting in line for her allotted rations of food, basic necessities (like soap, shampoo, toilet paper, etc.). I wish she didn't have to go back to Cuba so soon; I'm pleased to see my mother happy to see her for the time she is with us.

Derrick continues to be a part of my life. I haven't

been able to spend too much time with him since my grandmother has been here. Gary called me today. I really like him because he makes me laugh.

I worked today. I saw three patients. Homecare has been really good to me by giving me light assignments. I shouldn't be working, but I need the money!

August 16, 1990

My grandmother is gone, back to Cuba. She will be missed. She left ten days ago. While she was here, my roommate moved out without paying me for utilities or giving me any notice. His brother and nephew had just been here for ten days, too. He has visited before. My roommate really let me down because I trusted him

Wednesday, September 5, 1990

Gary invited me to go away with him for a weekend! I could sure use a vacation. His ex-roommate is getting married in Naples, Florida, and Gary is the best man. We will be staying at a hotel for three nights. I can't wait! I think I'm even going to have my own room. He tells me I don't have to spend a dime. I'm so excited! The only thing is, I can't figure *him* out. I mean, whether he likes me as more than a friend, or what. He is so nice and polite that I don't know whether he asked me on this trip because he wants to know me better or because he just wants to go with a friend. I guess I'll find out. I have got to make my mind up about Derrick. It's only a matter of time before the decision gets made.

I want to work so badly. I must take care of this body. I tell myself everything will work out; I just have to have faith. God is watching over me. I pray, not for a cure, but for strength to handle whatever comes my way.

My mom moved in with me last week. She is my new roommate. Luckily, we have a good relationship. She again is showing me sacrifices a mom makes for her child. I am sure it was tough to leave her home (she's renting it now) for *me*.

I'm so excited about my trip to Naples with Gary.

Tuesday, September 25, 1990

We just got back from Naples on Sunday. We had a fabulous time! We stayed at the Registry Hotel. What a beautiful place! I felt like a princess. I had my own room next to Gary's. Anyway, they valet parked the car, which I drove (Gary's car). The lobby was gorgeous, as well as our rooms.

Friday night we went to the Ritz for the wedding rehearsal (that hotel is beautiful as well); the following night, we went to dinner. There were twelve of us. Judging from the smiles and laughs, we all really enjoyed ourselves. Gary appeared comfortable with his friends. I was affectionately proud to be his date. It appears as though his friends sincerely care about him.

The next day we ordered room service from our separate rooms for breakfast. Then I went to Gary's room and helped him to complete his tuxedo attire. He looked handsome. The wedding was at 2:00 p.m. It went well, as well as the reception. Gary carried me on his lap in his wheelchair when I tired as we made our way through the hotel, which seemed enormous.

The next day he bought me a t-shirt and miniskirt at the gift shop. He wheeled me around in his lap in his wheelchair, and we took pictures in the hotel lobby. I loved riding in his lap! Overall, it was a wonderful trip.

It's finally come to an end with Derrick. We haven't been seeing each other much anyway—only at the gym on occasion. It's easy to go back; I'm vulnerable. I'm lonely. Mistakes are there to learn from, though, not to repeat!

5

CONFUSED

November 14, 1990

I really like this guy Rick. He seems to care about me. I met him at the gym. He's a little taller than me, with dark brown hair, brown eyes, and he's a body builder. We have so much in common! Well, except for the body-building part; I just like to do my best to keep fit. We even have the same birthday! He is eight years older than me. We actually have our houses painted the same colors, and our furniture choices are similar as well. We both drive red sports cars, we're both in the medical field, and we never run out of things to talk about. Derrick is going crazy. We all work out at the same gym (awkward!).

December 26, 1990

Christmas was the pits. It definitely could have been better. I sort of stopped seeing Rick, because he's not sure how he feels about me. I was really falling for him and, just when I thought he felt the same, he stopped calling me and told me he didn't want to lead me on. *What?* The multiple sclerosis diagnosis I have been given has caused him to question his attraction to me. "This is me, *all* of me. This is the whole package," I tell him, looking at him with raised eyebrows, as if he just wasted more of my precious time by encouraging me to be with him. "Just go," I tell him. I tell him I don't want to see him anymore, and what does he do? He calls me twice as much! I don't think he likes me to tell him to leave me alone. He says he really likes me. He says it's hard to tell me he loves me because of the MS.

It's hard to say good-bye to Derrick. It's easier to go back to what I am familiar with, even though I've already let him go. I don't *need* somebody, I *want* to be able to see whomever I want without having to deal with MS at the same time. Life can be so unfair. If it wasn't, I wouldn't have MS, I think. . . . I guess. . . . I'm confused. I have a hard time believing my life's course is based solely on my faith, my behavior during my time here. I don't get any satisfaction out of hurting others. So these physical impairments I experience as a result of having MS couldn't possibly be a result of any cruelty I've imposed on others.

On Sunday, Christmas Eve, I went to Raul's for a dinner that my mom made (she continues to care for him as his breathing becomes more difficult).

Christmas Day I went with my Lakeland friend to his home. That was very nice. We ate lunch and opened gifts. He had been thoughtful enough to have a gift for me. What I remember about the time we spent together is how at *ease* I felt during the short time we shared.

I saw Derrick briefly each day. Rick has been calling throughout the holidays as well. I think he *loves* me— kind of scary, huh?

I saw Rick on Christmas Eve. He gave me a necklace, with a heart-shaped charm with a diamond in it. It's difficult to accept such a gift. It's a bit puzzling to be given it by someone who sends me mixed signals about his feelings for me!

New Year's Day, January 1, 1991

Last night, after seeing Rick at work (at St. Mary's Hospital), I went to Raul's house, where my mother was. He has, as I keep writing, been very ill with increased breathing difficulty. Today, he went to the doctor, who diagnosed him with pneumonia, but Raul refused to go to the hospital. I was worried about him, so I thought I should see him to assess him and do my best to convince him to be admitted to the hospital to receive much needed medication. He was finally admitted to WRMC His arterial blood gases were extremely bad. I'm relieved he's in the hospital. I pray his condition improves. He recently quit smoking after many years.

That's a tough habit to quit, but I seriously think he didn't have a choice.

I visited him at the hospital. He appeared in improved condition compared to yesterday, although he continues to struggle with breathing, the course of COPD advancing as expected.

Following up on my night with Rick, I had the best New Year's Eve I can remember. I met him at his house after his work. It was about 11:00 p.m. His home has a park across the street. We went out to the gazebo with a bottle of champagne and celebrated the New Year there. We watched and heard fireworks from all around us! Then we went back into his house and danced for about an hour. We had the stereo on loud, like a night club. We kept making silly jokes about all the "imaginary" people at our party.

We truly enjoyed ourselves. He tells me now how he is telling everyone at work about it. He also says he's *crazy* about me. That gives me goose bumps! He wants me to have dinner with him tomorrow night. I can't wait!

January 10, 1991

I'm so in love! Rick told me he loves me! I won't see him tonight, he's working; that's okay—I need a good night's sleep.

Fortunately, the MS hasn't been showing its ugly face. I told Rick it's because I'm so happy. I don't know what else to write. I wish I didn't have MS, and then everything would be perfect.

February 4, 1991

I've been feeling great. Aside from a bladder infection, which is now gone, my vision is not causing me any problems.

Sunday, July 28, 1991

Wow, I didn't know I would have so much trouble writing. It's barely legible. My right arm is weak (I have difficulty holding a pen). I'm walking clumsily, as if I was a toddler. I dare to tell myself how much I hate this MS disease. I also tell myself I have to be strong.

It all started about a week ago and has slowly gotten worse. At first I thought I'd worked out too hard at the gym, but I hadn't done anything out of the ordinary. I know I haven't been sleeping well, because Rick and I broke up on Thursday, but the last two nights I slept okay.

The night before last, the pain in my right arm was so severe, I couldn't move it. I was home alone. I'll probably go to Dr. Millan's office tomorrow if this doesn't improve.

Wednesday, July 3, 1991

I was admitted to WRMC on Monday. I'm currently receiving ACTH intravenously. I haven't noticed any improvement. Today I feel as though my left side is getting worse—not my left arm, but my left leg is buckling a lot. My right side remains weak.

Thursday, August 1, 1991

I feel a tiny bit better, although my writing remains sloppy. I have been told by Dr. Millan that I have an active lesion at spinal vertebra C6–C7, which is causing my symptoms. We just have to hope I go into remission. Everyone has been supportive, including Rick. I'm scared, but I have to keep up my spirits—doctor's orders.

I'm listening to Rick's Walkman, hearing a song that makes me feel like jumping out of bed and dancing. I'm in shock. What if I could never go dancing again? It's like getting diagnosed all over again. What if I'm alone? I hear Rick tell me he will be there for me (easy to say, hard to believe). He doesn't know what he's in for. I have to rely on myself to get through this. I'm scared. I just didn't like the look on Dr. Millan's face when he told me about the MRI.

6

NOW WHAT?

Monday, August 5, 1991

I'm finally home today after eight days at WRMC. My writing has returned to normal. My right arm remains weak, but I can hold a pen now. My walking continues to be difficult. My right thigh is slightly stronger, but my gait is uncoordinated. I'm having a walker delivered today. I think it would be wise to use it to ambulate when I'm home alone. I have to believe I will go into remission from this attack, as I have in the past. I'm scared. Sometimes I just need to cry. There are so many things I want to do. I know I am fortunate in that I have a lot of support, but when it comes down to it, it's all up to *me*. I've got to be patient with walking. I'm going to get physical therapy as an outpatient at WRMC.

Rick and I have had our problems and arguments these past couple of weeks, but he is there for me now. I don't want to rely on him in case he up and runs, again. I tell him he doesn't have to be with me, but he says he wants to.

Derrick called me yesterday, when I was in the hospital. I was surprised to hear from him. He'd heard I was in the hospital, so he called because he said he was worried about me. That's nice. I appreciate the concern, but I hadn't heard from him in several months. My main concern is *me* right now. That may sound selfish, but I need to take care of myself so I don't have to depend on others.

August 11, 1991

As for the MS, my legs are fatigued. I overdid the walking yesterday, but I feel great otherwise. I mean, at least I'm walking!

I hope to see Allan tomorrow. He makes me feel good, safe, and comfortable. He is always there for me. That must be why I married him.

August 27, 1991

Today was *not* a good day. My dad and stepmother (Rosalinda) came over. Dad gave me a check for my health insurance and some meds. It felt good to get some things off my chest—for example, why does my father avoid me when I'm hospitalized? Rosalinda said he only visited her once when she had surgery. I get it. So hospitals tend to make Daddy uncomfortable. They are no joy for his daughter (me) either.

The day turned bad when I went to the dentist this afternoon. I haven't been in two and a half years because I couldn't afford it. I found out I have four cavities! Wonderful! That means about two hundred dollars' worth of fillings. I never had cavities as a child.

I went to a party on Peanut Island on Saturday with Derrick and his friend. I wanted to stay home, but he insisted it would be just as friends and he knew I would enjoy being around other people. I had a great time. Derrick was kind to me. He carried me piggy back on his back when my legs tired. He also set up an umbrella so I wouldn't spend too much time in the sun. I'm glad I went. At first, I was hesitant to be in public with Derrick, but then I thought, What have I got to lose? I wanted to go and I knew he wouldn't think of me as a burden. I had lots of fun. Besides, I'm not doing anything wrong. I never cared what other people thought of me any way. I know better. It's a good idea to avoid doing anything you know you will regret.

Rick left a message on my answering machine. I guess someone had told him I was with Derrick this weekend. Maybe if he thinks Derrick and I are back together, it will make it easier for him to forget about me. I don't know. I'm so tired. I haven't been sleeping well since we broke up, *again*, two weeks ago.

My mother is on vacation for a week with Raul, who

continues to benefit from her love for him, regardless of his treatment towards her. His COPD is slowly deteriorating as he struggles to breathe, desperately tries to control it. It *sucks* not being in control. They left yesterday; it's nice to have my house to myself. I am grateful for this home that I can call mine.

Sunday, September 1, 1991

Today was a good day. . .sort of. I didn't sleep well last night. Rick called me at 1:30 a.m. We talked for two hours, and then I hung up on him. It started out nice, with him telling me how much he missed me and how much he loved me. Then he started in about me seeing Derrick, and I didn't want to hear it. I can't help but think that the reason he is telling me these things and feeling so hurt is because I'm not falling apart. I have to be careful about whom I trust during tough times. I need someone to be supportive and mature. No more high school games: I need a *man*. I can't go through this breakup again. I can't get *sick* again. I must take care of this one time, one chance, body I have been entrusted with. If I don't, who will? Who actually cares about me more than me? No one else should. People see you as you see yourself. I see myself as someone—it could have been anyone, but it was me. I was randomly selected to live with MS. I see it almost like a dare. It's a challenge given to me. Now what am I going to do about it? I don't want others to pity me. I don't want to decide how

others see me. I know I can only control *my* behavior.
So I continue to control that which I can, *me*. I didn't
ask for this disease. So I smile and go through each day
as best I can.

Rick tells me he will go to counseling to help deal
with the unpredictability of living with MS. I think if
he meant it, he should have mentioned it before he left,
not after. I don't mean to be so heartless about him, but
I was so in love and tried so hard to make it work that I
feel utterly betrayed by all this. What's really ironic is
that both Rick and Derrick talk about marrying me, loving me, etc. I almost feel like not talking to either one
of them. This is way more stress than I'm willing to
deal with right now. Um, hello, guys, I'm kind of focusing on *healing?*

Wednesday, September 4, 1991

Today was an okay day. I can't believe I slept until
11:30 this morning. I felt like I could have slept all day.
I went to physical therapy at 1:00 p.m. I'm doing great.
My strength isn't back yet, but I have faith, and at least
I'm walking! Walking is important to me because everyone else walks without thinking about it. They take for
granted what I have so much difficulty doing. It's *normal*
to walk! I just want to be normal. I mean I *am* normal.
This could be anyone. It just happens to be me. Look at
me. People tend to look away. I think they feel as
though, if this could happen to me, it could happen to

them. That's a tough thought for them to deal with during this thing called life. I'm just living my life the best I can with what I've got. Walking or not, I must believe I am much more than that, more than a walking human being. After all, that's how I see myself. That's how I want for others to see me.

A lot has happened these past two days. Monday was Labor Day. Rick came over at 11:00 a.m. We hadn't seen each other in three weeks. He said he was miserable and wanted to make things work between us. He went on to tell me he understands why I was seeing Derrick, and he blames himself for it. He also says he wants to make a commitment and he wants us to live together and eventually get married. That's a lot to swallow!

And anyhow, wait a minute—isn't that another way of saying, "Stop dating other guys?" I was, and still am, so confused. I was just getting myself adjusted to being without him, and he comes back to me saying what I wanted to hear three weeks ago. I'm not ready to jump back into a relationship like that and run the risk of getting hurt again. I won't confront the issue now. People only treat you the way you let them.

Anyway, Al, an old friend from school, came over in the afternoon, about half an hour after Rick left my house. His visit was great. He showed me a video of when he did some amateur standup comedy. He's funny, plus he's nice to talk to. How refreshing. It's nice to have a visit from a friend. We talked a little about his girlfriend, a little about my relationship issues. We just talked and laughed; it was worth smiling about, and just what I *needed*.

September 6, 1991

I'm feeling good today. My MS seems to be okay. I want to say it's under control, but that's pushing it. My right leg keeps buckling under me when I'm standing or walking. But Julie, my physical therapist, says that's because my hamstrings are stronger than my quads. I need to work on those quads!

Rick is speaking to a counselor about us and other issues. I guess he's serious about how he feels about me. I mean, that takes guts! I'm sure it's easier to walk away from me. Who wants to deal with this headache? I think that's how *I* feel sometimes. *I* want to walk away. Heck, I just want to *walk!* I laugh at myself occasionally. I have to. I'm all I've got, always. I must keep a positive attitude for my own benefit.

September 27, 1991

I feel good. Samantha and I have been passing out pamphlets for the MS 150 bike tour, so I'm kind of tired. I'm a member of the board for the MS Society now.

October 21, 1991

I had my first board meeting last night. That went well.

I went to October Fest on Saturday night with Derrick (just friends). We had a good time. He carried me on his back when I fatigued. We danced a little. We had to do the chicken dance! Oh, did I mention Rick and I broke up? This is too much stress for me to handle. I'm glad to get my mind off relationship stuff and have fun.

I've been going to church since Rick and I broke up. It's the best thing I've done in a long time—I mean, going to church. I've met many kind people. I know it's easy to say breaking up was the best thing I've done, but the way I think of it, as I've written before, is that people treat you the way you let them. I feel I can either let someone continually hurt me, or I can chose to be treated with respect and return the behavior. Wow, then *I'm* in control!

Wednesday, October 30, 1991

I miss Rick. We talked on the phone today and basically decided he would give me more time to think about us. He says he loves me a lot and, when I'm ready, he said, "I'll be there." That means a lot to me. Now what? I need to make a decision before the MS shows up again and occupies my mind with thoughts about this illness. This life stuff is getting complicated! I think I'm growing up.

November 7, 1991

I have to be in Boca Raton at 6:00 a.m. on Saturday for the bike tour. Rick is concerned that it will aggravate the MS, because it is so early. Yes, Rick keeps calling me. We talk. I keep living my life without relying on others. Anyway, I can understand the concern, but when is he going to learn that I am one stubborn cookie and I'm going to do what I want anyway? If I don't feel well, I won't go. I'm learning how the MS affects me *every day*.

The bike tour was this weekend. I went alone. It was a lot of fun. The day ended with a party at J. Dickenson Park in Hobe Sound. When I got home, I had to use the wheelchair to prepare dinner because I was wiped out. At least the wheelchair made it possible for me to get my food! I don't *want* to use it, but I must focus on the positive. I had a fun, full, active day!

On Sunday, the bike tour continued, but I didn't go until noon. On my way, my tire came off of my car! That's not the first time that's happened to me. My rims don't fit properly on my RX7. The lug nuts just pop off, and, luckily, the tire didn't leave from under my car! I ended up having to get new rims yesterday—more money to spend that I don't have, but necessary.

I had a good day today! I worked for the first time in a couple of months. We got a pay raise to work weekends. I really need the money to pay for my new rims. Thank God for credit cards! They're how I got those rims. And now, of course, I need the money to pay off the credit cards!

Sunday, November 17, 1991

I'm tired. I woke up early today to go to church. I'm glad I went. After church I went to lunch with some of the people from Sunday school (a.k.a., singles). I enjoy these times. No pressure to do or be anything but me.

November 5, 1991

My mother is at Good Samaritan Hospital for voluntary surgery. She should be discharged in a couple of days. I want so badly to purchase a recliner for her for Christmas. I was going to charge it. She deserves it, but neither of us will be able to afford it. Rick suggested I ask my sister if she wanted to go in on it with me. She and her boyfriend agreed to pay for half! My mom will be so happy when she gets home from the hospital! The chair is already in her room! Rick said he will also help with the cost. He's been nice. I'm still cautious, emotionally. He actually took responsibility for the arguments between us lately, though. We are planning to spend the holidays together. So, yes, we're seeing each again, even though I rarely give guys another chance. He is persistent! We are closer than we have been in a long time. It must be that holiday spirit!

Monday, January 13, 1992

Rick asked me to marry him. . .sort of. Well, we started talking about living together, and then we talked about marriage. He's saying all the right things. It all sounds so perfect. He's serious, really serious. I'm still cautious, protecting myself emotionally. We have a fantastic time together. The holidays were great, better than last year.

Then we got the flu! Rick was at home for a week. He went back to work today. I'm still sick. I haven't said anything, but my left leg is buckling. I need to rest and get over the flu. So Rick wants to marry me. I must give this serious thought.

Mom has been home. She is feeling good. She loves her new recliner!

Wednesday, January 15, 1992

Yesterday, Rick and I went to look at engagement-wedding rings. We are looking forward to building a life together. We have so much in common, and we want the same things in a marriage—companionship, love, and a best friend. While looking at rings, one of the salesmen mentioned his wife had MS. I can't believe we met him while looking for a ring. He was very encouraging and optimistic about having a spouse with MS. The salesman said, "Keep the faith." He's right. You just have to believe there will someday be a cure and think positive until they do. If you don't, you have lost the fight. That's how I see it. It's a fight. I must be as productive with my energy in spite of this diagnosis.

March 31, 1992

It's almost impossible to recount everything that has occurred in these past couple of months, but I guess I should start with the most important. Rick and I are engaged! It was so romantic. We went to Orlando a couple of weeks ago. He had to take an exam (part of continuing education for his therapy license), so he said we might as well go to Epcot and enjoy our weekend. The first night we stayed in what is known as a "dive," a motel close to the college, also known as "Motel Hell" to some. We had no hot water, rock-hard pillows, lumpy beds, and an unpleasant smell like an old building. To top off our stay, I forgot my shampoo for my long dark brown hair! We were so sleepy, and his exam was the next day, so we hoped for a rapid night in that place!

That was Friday night. Rick took his test Saturday morning, and then we went to our real hotel. He'd made reservations at a Disney resort, The Royal Plaza. It was beautiful. Our room was complete with a king-size bed and. . . shampoo! Rick made dinner reservations in Epcot at the restaurant in Mexico called San Miguel. We went there that night. We wore jeans with a nice shirt. The weather was cool (for Florida). The restaurant was dark, romantic, quite a change from our evening the night before.

I remember glasses of wine at the table. How thoughtful, I thought; what a classy atmosphere. Dinner was delicious. I couldn't remember Mexican food prepared so tastefully. After a wonderful dinner, we were looking forward to an extraordinary dessert. And there came the plate with dessert choices. The *maître d'* asked, "Do you see something you like?" As I considered by choice, I noticed a small jewelry box with a diamond ring! I was looking at Rick in disbelief when he got out of his chair, onto one knee, took my hand in his, and asked if I'd marry him.

With tears in my eyes and in complete disbelief, I said, "Yes!" The entire restaurant, full of customers, began to applaud! Rick had gone to so much trouble to make that weekend special—and it was.

Wednesday, May 6, 1992

I have been feeling well for quite a while, until now. I'm struggling with my breathing, feeling I can't catch my breath. I don't know what it is. I just know there are times when I'm SOB (short of breath). Today was one of those days. I can't remember being comfortable breathing at all today. I just want the feeling to go away. I saw a pulmonologist the other day. He said it's not asthma and to just relax. I hate it when doctors brush off complaints like that. He's *not* taking me seriously. How *belittling*.

Friday, May 8, 1992

I feel so *fatigued*—writing requires such effort. I saw Dr. Millan yesterday. I told him about the SOB and fatigue, and also described how my legs have been buck-ling under me. It's really weird how they feel when they do that. It is not that my muscles aren't strong enough since I work out at the gym at least once a week, and I don't have any numbness in my legs. It's just that they feel like they want to collapse. The SOB has improved somewhat, although I was noticeably out of breath this morning.

Rick has been good to me, bless his heart. He doesn't like to see me suffer. Me neither! Sometimes I cry be-cause I feel his pain. It's ironic how he hurts for me. We are so alike at times, though so many times we are not, and those are the times that I find most challenging. Those are the times I feel alone and abandoned in this struggle to be an ordinary person.

I told Dr. Millan I want to walk down the aisle at our wedding. It frightens me that my legs are buckling. I've never been this way before. I want to fix it and for-get about it! I'm afraid to walk, because I might not be able to control my legs and I don't want to fall and get hurt.

Dr. Millan says the SOB could be because I'm so fa-tigued that my respiratory muscles are fatigued, but we don't want to assume the worst and say that the MS is affecting my respiratory receptor sites. I don't want to assume anything! I just want to concern myself with wedding plans, not breathing plans! Once again MS gets my attention. Once again my life plans are put on hold. No time for feeling sorry for myself. I have a wedding to plan! I will pick myself up (*ha!*) and do my best to be optimistic. I can—I mean *will*, do this! It would be so easy to give up. I don't do *easy* well! It's always easy to do the wrong thing. I would not benefit anyway.

Dr. Millan says I am definitely displaying signs and symptoms of an exacerbation, but he doesn't want to put me in the hospital, and I don't either! So now, it has been proven that treatment as soon as possible is best.

Sunday, May 10, 1992

Today is Mother's Day. I went to church with my mom and Rick went to Miami to see his.

Yesterday, I spent the majority of the day in pain from head to toe but mostly in my legs. I might as well be walking into a burning building. I notice my right arm more than my left. I took an "ice bath" yesterday and the day before. My idea—I just wanted the burning to stop! That usually helps the burning in my legs, but the pain is also achy. I haven't discovered a treatment for that. No more drugs!

I felt a little better by last night, so Rick and I went out to dinner. Going to bed that night, the achy feeling persisted, but I managed to fall asleep, only to be awakened at 3:00 a.m. from a nightmare about not being able to control my bladder! I woke up and rushed to the bathroom, only to find that I couldn't go. I mean, I was able to go a little bit, but nothing like what I'd dreamt!

Anyway, as I rushed to the bathroom at 3:00 a.m., I noticed my left leg had slight numbness in the thigh. Right now, I'm experiencing what resembles pins and needles on the top of my left foot. Rick has been rubbing oils on my legs for the pain. That always feels good. My breathing has improved considerably. I still don't feel, though, that I can raise my voice much above a whisper.

May 11, 1992 Monday

I've been admitted to St. Mary's Hospital. I continue to have pain throughout my body, radiating from both shoulder blades down the arms. I am so fatigued. I feel I have no energy to do even the simplest of things. My left eye hurts at random, like lightning strikes. Dr. Millan encouraged me to be admitted because "the sooner we catch it [the exacerbation, he means] and treat it, the better." I am reaching my limit of being a patient instead of a nurse, but I respect my doctor, so I proceed.

Saturday, May 16, 1992

I'm going home tomorrow! I'm not fixed. But I am improved and ready to go home.

Tuesday, May 19, 1992

I came home Sunday with Rick. I just took it easy all day. My mom made dinner and key lime pie and brought it over to Rick's house, and we all ate it together.

Yesterday was our birthday. We had a good day.

We were just grateful I was out of the hospital—that was our birthday present. Times like this allow us to realize what really matters and what a gift really is. They also show me who will be there for me during difficult times.

Monday, June 22, 1992

I went from a fabulous weekend to a miserable Monday. The bottoms of my feet are numb; it feels as if I'm wearing shoes. Rick and I did a lot this weekend, and I know I overdid it again. We went canoeing at John Dickenson Park in Hobe Sound, and took walks on the nature trail, and went to the top of the tower to see the ocean from there. I used an umbrella to block the sun. It was so hot—90-ish weather.

Wednesday, June 24, 1992

No improvement with my feet yet. They are uncomfortably numb on the soles of my feet. My calves feel weak when I walk. I want this disease to go away. Yesterday, I banged my left foot on the decorative landscaping pebbles out in front of Rick's house and cut my little toe. I want this to stop. I need a break from this Life. I have MS, and I am fighting for the ability, correction, and challenge of being independent and self-sufficient, but it seems close to impossible when I am continually bombarded with symptoms over which I have no control. What to do. . .I must keep a clear, confident mind. I have to stay focused on thoughts that will help me, not hurt me.

Monday, June 29, 1992

I can't believe I have the *chicken pox!* That would explain my MS symptoms for the past week! I hope the MS improves when the chicken pox goes away. How did I get it? I was with my niece, Hanna, two weeks ago when my mom, who was babysitting her, went with me to look at wedding dresses. The next day, Hanna broke out with the chicken pox.

I have a slight fever, but I'm doing O.K. I'm taking Zorax to lessen the anticipated symptoms, which is no fun as an adult!

Saturday, January 23, 1992

As for the MS, these past few months I've encountered a few bouts with bladder retention and SOB, both of which have subsided for now. A couple of weeks ago, the center of my lower lip went numb. I occasionally would bite my lip. *Ouch!* The numbness lasted five days and then disappeared.

As of late, the right side of my lower lip is numb and has gotten number the last three days. This morning the top of my left foot was numb, and this numbness has progressed over the past two hours to up to my left knee. This is *not good.* I've been sleeping so much, I'm surprised the MS is acting up. Who can figure.

Rick wants to go to the fair tonight. That makes me nervous, especially because we are meeting some friends there. I'm not feeling well, but I don't want to keep everyone from walking all over the fair grounds. Oh, well, I have nothing to feel bad about. It's not my fault I have MS.

About my house—I moved out in July and moved in with Rick. I finally rented it out in October.

Tuesday, January 25, 1993

We didn't go to the fair on Saturday. We wanted to, but my MS has gotten worse over the past two days. When I woke up yesterday, both my legs were numb from my waist down to my toes. My right side feels heavier than my left. I haven't had this much heaviness in a long time. It's no fun lugging around ankle weights; that might as well be what I'm doing! I'm afraid it may be an exacerbation, but I just want to keep an eye on it to see if it improves on its own. Can I say *denial?* Maybe I should just call it *wishful thinking?* I'm optimistic, though. My feet feel so cold, but they're not; they just feel that way. I'm emptying my bladder, thank god.

Thursday, January 27, 1993

They admitted me to St. Mary's again at 12:00 p.m. today. Rick ran into Dr. Millan last night in the hospital. He told Rick I should have been admitted already. The sooner it's caught, the less likely it will be permanent. I already knew that, but I wanted believe it would get better so I could get out of here! In fact, my thighs are a little numb again. At least I'm in a private room in Pediatrics—and I kinda like it! It's so cheery and quiet.

Friday, January 28, 1993

They're moving me to a private room on an adult floor. That's okay; at least it's private. It is complete with grab bars, among other features for disabled. To me, it's a priceless opportunity to be independent.

Unfortunately, my condition worsens. I had trouble with my breathing this morning; deep breaths are difficult for me. Rick gave me oxygen via nasal cannula upon getting the order from Dr. Millan. That lessened the work of breathing for me. Work? Breathing? Breathing is not *supposed* to be work! My legs feel heavier. Sometimes they feel hot, too, though at others they feel ice cold.

Saturday, January 29, 1993

I slept like a log last night. I really needed uninterrupted sleep. I'm dragging both legs when I ambulate. My legs don't seem as numb, but they are weak, or weaker. This is the pits.

Rick has been good to me. He has other concerns involving his family but he puts me first, though he doesn't have to.

Sunday, January 31, 1993

I don't understand why I am so much weaker today compared to yesterday. It's the lowest point in my battle with this illness. It's scary. I wanted to go home today to watch the Super Bowl, but we are just going to watch it here. Yes, I said Super Bowl. I actually enjoy watching football now that Rick has explained it to me. We often hate what we don't understand.

Tuesday, February 2, 1993

Today I feel a little depressed, although my spirits have been up throughout my hospitalization. I've been riding in the halls in my wheelchair and meeting my neighbors with a smile on my face to maybe bring some cheer to their hospitalization, and it has a positive effect on me too when they smile back. Smiles are contagious. Everyone seems so nice.

Rick and I had a fun time watching the Super Bowl on Sunday night. He was so cute—he brought chips, salsa, and pizza, plus beer (*oops*—beer!). Not for me; I don't like beer, and besides, I'm on medication. He just wanted to give me the *atmosphere*, a little touch of a party. I call it *mental* medicine!

Tuesday, February 23, 1993

I was discharged on February 6 with a sore throat, which I am currently on antibiotics for. I was so happy to go home. MS continues to remind me of its presence.

My feet are still uncomfortably cold. The coldness feels exaggerated; if my feet are cold, I perceive them to be *extremely* cold.

What I really wanted to write about is that we set our wedding date for May 29! We've booked the church, and I've found my wedding dress! At this rate we'll have the wedding ready to go by next week!

Monday, March 8, 1993

Wow! We just booked a honeymoon to *Rome!* I have to pinch myself to see if I'm dreaming. *Ouch!* It *must* be real. Sure, Rick was talking about Niagara Falls, but I said, for the money we would spend there, why not go to another country? He told me he would show me the world while I was still walking. Not walking has *never* been a part of my life plan! It's a good thing, too, because things have rarely gone according to that plan.

I've been feeling practically as close to normal as before. Now I'm preoccupied with all the planning. I guess you could say I feel *almost* normal, with normal problems. *Love it!*

7

MIAMI

Monday, September 20, 1993

Here I am at Jackson Memorial Hospital under Dr. Sheremata's care. I was admitted Friday after much resistance. I did not want to go in. I was in St. Mary's Hospital only last month (August 2–9) with Dr. Millan. I was also in the hospital three weeks before our wedding. That's right; Rick and I were married May 29. The wedding was beautiful! I didn't know how I would feel on my wedding day, since I had been hospitalized weeks before—*yuck!* Thankfully, everything went well, and. . .I *walked!*

That's right, I walked down the aisle. Our honeymoon was awesome, too! We really did go to Italy, where we saw everything! I even took a wheelchair I had borrowed from the MS Society, but I just parked it in the closet of our hotel room and was able to enjoy our

Our wedding, May 29, 1993

trip, knowing I had it as back up for possible "bad" days.

We landed in Rome after a very, very, very long flight, wearing the *Italy Just Married* t-shirts that we'd had printed.

After heading to our lovely, spacious hotel room, we crashed on the bed. We were *so* sleepy from the flight with uncomfortable airplane seats and way too few bathrooms. The time change didn't help, either. Nevertheless, after a quick siesta, we headed out to explore the streets close to our hotel and found a lunch stop. We enjoyed a real Italian meal in Italy. Just the *aroma* of actual Italian food is mouthwatering.

We were there for ten days. We started in Rome, then made our way to Florence, Pisa, Venice, Naples, the Isle of Capri, Sorrento, and Pompeii. I can't believe I walked in Pompeii. Now I understand why they call the country *Sunny Italy*. It's hot! I walked all the time, though, and I felt great.

It's *now* that I don't feel so hot, I mean well. I have had a heavy right leg since Labor Day weekend (September 4), when Rick and I went to Daytona to see his sister's family (husband and three girls). Their oldest daughter had recently turned seven. The party was outside, for the most part. I remained indoors, because the weather was warm and, knowing I can only challenge this body so much, I did my best to keep cool. I lcok healthy, but my invisible symptoms of pain, numbness, fatigue, and frustration with these symptoms dominate all thoughts of having fun. Regardless, I appeared ccntent with the situation. After all, I didn't want to be a party pooper. I never do.

So here I am, a patient once again. My right leg got heavy, weak, and numb. Of course there is more. My bladder has been a problem with retention and frequency/ hesitancy. And stay with me—there's *more*. I've had trouble focusing and reading. My eyes are troubling me as well: Everything appears to jump around. I might as well be on a trampoline, reading a book.

September 26, 1993

Dr. Sheremata sticks his head in my doorway from time to time and says, with a smile on his face, "Keep smiling!" Words are powerful. I need to be reminded of this basic option, which I can control! I slept like a rock last night. I've been getting 5 mg of Valium at bedtime. Dr. Sheremata says it helps relax my bladder, so I don't get up as often. To me, it just relaxes me in general! I've had 2 MRIs done during my stay at Jackson—brain and c-spine. The MRIs showed worsening of the disease.

I want a magic wand, and *poof!* it's all gone. I don't want to deal with this anymore. Oh, I'm still smiling. I have to. Maybe I can disguise the emotions flooding my brain right now. Dr. Sheremata continues to tell me, "But this interferon is good stuff!" His smile is sincere. I trust him. I need to trust him. I pray this works for me. I don't pray for a cure, but for strength to handle whatever comes my way. I am fortunate to be his patient. There is a lottery to be on this medication, for which he was allotted sixty slots. I am one of those sixty. I am happy and uneasy at the same time, nervous about yet another med that I am unfamiliar with.

My stay here has been great. No one knows me as

Alys, Rick's wife; they just know me as Alys, and I like that. It makes me feel like an individual. If they like me, it's because of who I am. I feel normal again. No one judges me or criticizes me. No one pities me or feels sorry for me. They just treat me like a regular person who happens to have MS. The paramedics, from back when I had the ambulance rides I took to get MRIs done, keep popping in. They do wheelies in my wheelchair and tease me. More important, they get my mind off this hospitalization. They don't feel sorry for me, they're just nice. I miss being around people and dread going back home and being alone. Yes, I do want to go home—it's the being alone part I don't miss. I'm alone because I don't feel well, and I don't want to share that feeling with anyone. I don't find pleasure in sharing miserable times with others. No one benefits. These discussions are best left to my physician or other MSers who may understand, as well as relate to, what I'm experiencing.

The MS has taken that freedom of being who I want to be away and turned my life into including it in my plans.

So, here goes: my life plans including MS. I don't like it, but this is my life. I must make my life function for *me*. A slight grin appears on my face. Thinking positively, I remind myself, my MS has improved; I'm using a walker for short distances. I have decorated it with a smiley-face sticker and a lot of colorful ribbons all centered in the middle of the unattractive silver frame. I'm walking short distances down the hall. My feet get number as I walk, but I have to ambulate so I can get better. My balance has improved. My right leg buckles after a few steps, and it is still weaker than the left, but the ACTH has helped a lot. My vision has improved but less in the left eye. I can read now even though vision is slightly blurry in the left eye. My bladder issues have improved (amen). The fatigue was awful yesterday afternoon through evening, but that's probably because I've started ambulating and that wore me out. I believe I must move in order to remind my nerve cells and muscles how to function. If I don't, my body will give up and check out. I can't have that!

I have a kind med student, and I met a female med student from Hong Kong the other night who talked to me for like an hour and a half. It was great to have her company. As I said, everyone has been so friendly.

Wednesday, September 29, 1993

I had a student nurse last night who was a doll. She talks a lot but kept me company and made me laugh. She took me downstairs to the gift shop and cafeteria. She even took me outside for a short time. By the time I returned to my room, I was exhausted! All I did was sit in the wheelchair, and it still wore me out! Worth every moment, though. I'm up walking with the walker one to two times a day. I walk to just outside my room, but that's an improvement. I'm feeling better, and my strength has improved, but my feet get numb, like walking on golf balls. Dr. Sheremata says that's to be expected because I'm starting to be more active and the ACTH is being therapeutic. Whatever, I think to myself, I respect my doctor, so I comply. I do feel better, for whatever reason. I can't wait to see Rick today. I haven't seen him since Friday.

Monday, October 4, 1993

Dr. Sheremata was just in and said I can go home Friday! I really like him. He brings out the optimistic positive side of living with MS, for me anyway. It is hard to say anything good about living with a chronic illness. I guess it's even harder to be a physician treating a disease without being able to "fix" a patient.

That's three weeks in this place. I've been here a long time, receiving ACTH intravenously. Usually, it's about a week, but I think we did something longer for this illness. It was a bad attack, so I'm willing to do what I can to help me recover from this episode of a disease for which there is no cure.

My stay here has been quite bearable. I am grateful for this large room with many windows I was fortunate to get. Also, I have made many friends as well as meeting other people with MS, one of whom is going home today. She came from Port St. Lucie to see Dr. Sheremata. I have met patients from all over. We are all searching in vain for that certain someone with the secret cure to eliminate this troubling situation and allow us to continue our lives without MS.

Anyway, she took me downstairs tonight (she is walking). I got dinner from one of the restaurants. Rick takes me there sometimes, too. He came to visit yesterday.

My mom visited during the day, and my sister was here on Saturday with board games she'd brought from home. My dad and family (I now have a half-sister and half-brother, because my dad and stepmother had two children, who were also in our wedding party) were here as well.

I'm excited about starting the new medication. It should be any day now. I perceive it as *hope*. Dr. Sheremata says my body doesn't produce enough interferon according to some genetic tests he ran, so the Betaseron is really something I should benefit from (I hope—I *think* that's what he meant).

Who cares? I'm going home on Friday. I miss my house, my dog, my husband, etc. Dr. Sheremata says my husband is a lucky man. He says things that make me feel good about *me*. It doesn't even matter if he tells other patients the same things. I don't care. I just know he gives me positive, feel-good words. I'll take them!

October 7, 1993 Friday

Tonight is my last night at Jackson Memorial Hospital. It has been a descent visit. I have made a ton of friends with and without MS. I am looking forward to getting back to our house. I feel great. I'm really tired right now. It has been a busy day. I've been talking to everybody.

Tonight, I had a sort of party in my room (which I have decorated with pictures taped on the wall of family, house, pool, my dog, get-well cards, etc.). Plus I have flowers on the counter, table, wherever I can find a place for them. Some flowers may need to be disposed of, because they have been here for a while wilting but they are *flowers*! As I was saying, patients from the floor, and their visitors, gathered in my room. I was showing them my wedding album, which Rick brought the other day. The album is beautiful, and the photographer said he liked it so much he is making a copy to keep at his studio!

I'm glad Rick surprised me by bringing it. So I showed pictures, we talked about MS among other subjects, just talked and talked! I hope they enjoyed it as much as I did. The only thing missing were magic-cure cocktails!

I can't thank God enough. I have a lot to be grateful for. I feel good right now. See, it's not what problems we have; it's how we confront them. I believe this is what makes us different. I could feel sorry for myself and this hard time I'm going through, or I can see it as an opportunity to learn from and become a better, stronger person.

8

HOME AT LAST

Saturday, October 9, 1993

It feels good to be home! Rick surprised me with balloons, ribbons, and a welcome-home banner. It brought tears to my eyes. Of course so did seeing my happy, tail-wagging dog, Zubi. He was fluffy-clean and jumped in my lap as soon as he saw me. I feel good today, but it is an adjustment for me to be home. My hands are trembling terribly. My legs fatigue easily, so walking is very limited. I just have to pace myself and get to what I consider to be normal before starting the Betaseron.

I'm kind of nervous about the depressive side-effects, but I've told my family to watch for them, and I will be well aware if I'm not my usual happy self. Dr. Sheremata told me I shouldn't have any problem with depression or suicide (yikes!). I believe I can handle the flu-like symptoms. Dr. Sheremata says I'm an intelligent and highly motivated person and I should do fine on the drug. (See? More of that feel-good talk!)

The study used to approve the drug only involved about three hundred people, so I feel I'll be part of a continuing experiment with a drug that will be FDA approved. I guess I'm lucky to get to try it because so many people want to and can't, since there isn't enough supply for the demand. I'm lucky Sheremata chose me to be one of the ones he was allotted. Other people have to hope they get picked from the lottery. Sure, I can tell myself I'm like a lab rat, *or* I can focus on improving my condition, which may include experimenting with meds that offer a better outcome than no meds. I've done that already. I trust this doctor to treat my condition, which is not improving on its own.

Monday, January 24, 1994

I felt great during the holidays. I believe being happy has a huge impact on how I feel. I seem to feel better when I'm happy. Rick and I had a wonderful first Christmas as a married couple. We are doing better than I expected. I often hear about how the start of marriage can be difficult because change is difficult! That's how I look at marriage. Now, throw a wrench in it (MS) and, *bam!* it is more than anyone could have ever imagined. We get along well and listen to each other.

MS-wise, I feel as though I have recovered from that

awful exacerbation and returned to my previous self, but a tiny bit less.

Friday, February 4, 1994

I gave myself my first shot of Betaseron last night. It wasn't as bad as I imagined but I was achy and had chills. Still, I was prepared for much worse. I think I'm going to be okay with this drug. I just have to get through this first month; then the symptoms should subside.

February 5, 1994

Rick and I went to dinner tonight at R.J. Gators, and I saw someone from high school there. He said our ten-year reunion is coming up in June or July. I told him I hadn't received the invitation. I have not received many mailed items since I moved. He said he would give them my address, but, honestly, I'm not feeling much like a reunion. Isn't that awful? I take a moment to reflect on these past few years, and you know what? I don't think that it's reunion material for conversation! I feel I have had so many growing-up-too-fast issues that other classmates wouldn't or shouldn't have to confront at our age. I was originally looking forward to chatting with classmates about our lives post-graduation, but my plans were drastically altered by my uninvited guest.

I took my second shot of Betaseron tonight. It burns when it goes in, but the site looks better than before, not as red as last night. I feel good. I hope I have a good night.

We've been remodeling our kitchen. Rick and I put all the cabinets together, and now they are in the living room. When I agreed to move out of my home, he agreed that I could remodel his house to make it ours. Besides, I enjoy seeing what I can do with the space! I can't wait until Saturday, when we have them installed! (Once they were installed, they looked good enough for Home Depot to post a picture of our kitchen with the cabinets we purchased from them!) I have fun remodeling. Keeps my mind off the disease and focused on creativity, which can't be bad!

Sunday, February 6, 1994

I've been nauseated most of the day. I have no desire to eat or smell food, but I did manage to swallow a little lunch, followed by a small portion of dinner. I just think of food as medicine I have to eat. I have to get fuel into this body, so it can function to the best of its ability. This is something I can control!

April 1994

My great-aunt Tia Tina is at Hospice. She has been battling stomach cancer for months. Her second husband committed suicide at their home before her diagnosis. She has already confronted the cost of losing a loved one in Vietnam in 1969. Then, it was Billy, one of her two sons; her second, Tom, has survived. Now she has her own battle to fight. She is strong, brave, and I love her with all my heart.

Once we arrive and enter the hospice building, I feel the peaceful quiet atmosphere—a comfort for those that are cared for there. I'm walking with a cane today. My family is gathered in the sitting area provided in the center of the main room. When I am given the opportunity to visit her room, I approach the bed where she is resting with her eyes closed. She is beautiful. I am on her left side as my mother stands at her right. We are trying to keep the tears from falling from our moist eyes. I place my hand in Tia Tina's hand and whisper in her ear, "Tia Tina, it's Alys. I love you." She squeezes my hand. She is listening to me. I whisper, "You know, the suffering and pain you have been enduring, it's temporary, you only have it until you die. We will be pain free and dancing in heaven." My smile is gentle; my hold on her hand is tighter. I feel a stronger grip from her hand. I am certain she understands what I am saying.

After a few days, we attend the inevitable, her funeral. The service is beautiful as is the music playing from the album her deceased son made prior to his death in Vietnam. He was killed while he hovered in his helicopter above other brave Americans he attempted to rescue. His beautiful music plays on. His memory for me is minimal, as I was only three years old. Still, my thoughts of him, as well as his mother, will forever be embedded in my mind, as they should be. I am grateful my other second cousin, Tom, continues to remind me of the kind, loving family members they were. Lucky for me, he lives only a short distance from my home. Lucky for all of us, he was released from serving in the army upon the death of his brother.

I will forever be grateful for Tia Tina. She was a large part of the reason our family came to America. Her husband was serving in the army in the U.S.A., thus providing a smooth transition from Cuba for my family as Castro's dictatorship became more pronounced.

I think of her often—not only the way she was always affectionate with her Christmas gifts and the $5.00 check she would send each birthday, but of how she was consistently honest and kind to me and others. I don't believe her life turned out the way she envisioned. I recall my mother telling me she fainted when her son's body arrived in America. I can only imagine what she was feeling. I suppose her thoughts included what most of us would be thinking: *This is not fair.*

Thursday, July 27, 1995

I am depressed. I mean *really* depressed. It's hard for me to write that, but I want to capture my feelings in my journal and that's how I feel. I can't talk to Rick about it. I don't want to talk to anyone. I'm embarrassed and ashamed that I feel this way, and I don't want to let people down. I'm the one who is usually there for others to cheer them up and tell them to think positive. I must talk to someone in my *safe zone*. That would be someone I can let down my guard with, be myself, and not worry about being judged by them because they love me unconditionally. Immediately I think of my mom. I feel better already. Everyone should have a safe zone! One person can make a difference.

Since I started on the Betaseron, I haven't been in the hospital! I guess it has kept my disease under control.

Wednesday, December 6, 1995

I can't believe I'm in the hospital once more. It's my second day at Jackson Memorial. I'm glad I'm in a private room. I don't want to be here. At least my sister's husband, Steve, visits me occasionally. He cheers me up, he really does. He's funny. (He will go out of his way to see me, alone, later in Miami!)

Thursday, December 7, 1995

I have a temperature of 100.1, and I have been sneezing often today. My nose is stuffy. The resident ordered Sudafed for me, so I'm waiting for that to come up. I am miserable, but on a high note, I'm so glad I have my wheelchair now! I'm *free!* My wheelchair color is hot pink. I recall purchasing it many years ago for those long walking times that can be challenging for me. Now I can ride all around the floor. I met a woman with MS down the hall. She seemed like she would welcome a visit. I'm going to go by her room later.

Friday, December 8, 1995

Today was a good day. I'm feeling better, and I want to go home. Sleeping at night can be challenging, because that's when I'm given the ACTH intravenously, so I constantly have to use the restroom, but at least my bladder is capable of notifying me! It takes many nerve cells to control the bladder. That is why so many MS patients have symptoms involving it.

My dad called today. He just found out I was here? I guess we need better communicating skills in this family. I'm glad he called.

I just got back from getting my MRI of the brain. I go for a ride in an ambulance to get to the MRI center. That was my field trip for the day. Earlier, Rick was here and took me downstairs, where we went to a craft fair outside and looked around. At least I got to get out of the room and off the floor for a while. Besides, shopping is free!

Saturday, December 9, 1995

I had an MRI of the c-spine today. That's right, another field trip! I'm glad I met Gizabella, the woman with MS I wrote about earlier. She has been a pleasure to be with during these rough times in the hospital as opposed to being home and living life as a regular person with regular, everyday situations like waking up on time for work, eating breakfast, and getting dressed. Oh, that's right—I get to deal with those issues as well!

Sunday, December 10, 1995

Wow, what an emotional day. To begin with, my friend with MS left this afternoon. Then the residents on the floor wanted to see me walk for them (that was interesting). Then my mom visited along with her mom, Abuela Olga, and Raul, so we went downstairs and outside to get them food. Raul appears to be tolerating the long walk (of course I'm watching him!). I guess it's the nurse in me that remains concerned about his health. Then, Dr. Sheremata got here and surprised me with what he said. He told me, "Stop the Betaseron, because it is no longer working." He showed me the new lesions on my c-spine MRI. He continued, "I don't know how long you will be here, but the longer you stay, the better you will do." He also said he recommends that I start on recumbent Alpha–interferon. He told me I am producing antibodies to the Betaseron, rendering it useless. That's unbelievable but not unusual. He said I'd done better on it than most people. I'm uneasy about starting a new med *again*. So I talked to Scott Wood (a certified inhabitant of my safe zone). He tends to make me feel better. I think he is also on the same medication.

Anyway, my dad came this afternoon with his family, including his mother (my other grandmother). I introduced him to Dr. Sheremata. I told him I want him to know what *I'm* going through. I believe my dad genuinely loves me, so knowing I am hurting possibly gives him feelings of helplessness. Isn't that what we all feel about this disease?

My friends Sue and Samantha have been very supportive tonight by just being there for me. They call me often; Sue even wrote me a poem using my name! That means so much to me.

Monday, December 11, 1995

I had physical and occupational therapy today. I'm wiped out. I'm walking poorly now because I've had an active day, but I'm glad to move. Scott's mom called me today. She treats me as though she was *my* mom. It was great to hear from her. She is so nice to me. I was so glad to see Rick tonight, too. I miss him.

I have to relearn how to walk normally. I want to go home. I miss Zubi. I'm tired. Today was good but busy. My interpretation of "good" is being happy with my productive time. On days like that, it's easy to smile!

Monday, December 12, 1995

Today was a busy day too, starting with being awakened at 7:30 a.m. to get an evoke potential done. Then, I had more occupational therapy.

I am walking better. The numbness in my right leg

has decreased. I have been feeling improved in general these past few days. I had physical therapy-rehabilitation off the floor today. It was totally different from PT in my room. I worked out harder than I do in the gym. I'm beat! I want to go home.

Friday morning, December 15, 1995

I feel good this morning. Dr. Sheremata came by yesterday and said we are looking at this weekend for discharge! I'm limiting my activity this morning so I will do well at PT.

I got a call from our next-door neighbor. She said they started to pressure-clean the deck around the pool that we are having installed. The pool is great exercise for MS—that's why we're getting one. Maybe it'll be done for Christmas!

Friday night, December 15, 1995

I feel strong. I am excited to be going home tomorrow. Dr. Sheremata said absolutely no Christmas shopping. He said there are some bad viral flu bugs floating around, and he doesn't want me to catch anything to exacerbate my MS. He suggested I stay away from heavily populated areas—for example, *malls*. I haven't done any Christmas shopping. Oh, well. The good news is that I'm home for Christmas. It's funny how I view good news now; just knowing I'm going home is simple but joyful!

Friday, March 1, 1996

I feel sick right now, as if I have the flu, but I don't. I started the Alpha last night. I woke up at 2:00 a.m. with chills, headache, and body ache, miserable and sick. These are the flu-like symptoms associated with taking Alpha interferon; but Sheremata and Scott told me there'd be no side effects. These are worse than the ones from the Betaseron, which would burn occasionally going in. I continually remind myself of how every person with MS is different in the way they handle *everything!* No two are alike. Some are similar, but we are all unique, thus the name of this disease—multiple sclerosis (multiple scars). The scars can occur *anywhere* in the central nervous system. But these are side effects I'm experiencing, not MS symptoms. I'm so nauseated right now, I just want to throw up. I have a low-grade temp.

On the plus side, the injection didn't hurt at all going in.

I had wanted to avoid starting the Alpha because I was feeling so good, but I've been a little numb and quite fatigued lately, so I figured it was time. I was enjoying my time without meds to treat MS.

About Christmas: We had a wonderful Christmas Eve at our house with many family members from both of our families. Mom and Abuela Olga cooked the *lechon asado* (pulled pork), our traditional Cuban Christmas dinner. They cooked it because I had been discharged only the week before, and I wasn't feeling much like cooking—or walking for that matter. Sucked, because I enjoy cooking.

Our pool was finally finished about a month ago. I go in it sometimes because I can move without tremendous energy! Love it!

Tuesday, May 7, 1996

I am so out of breath. Taking my mail out to the end of the driveway is difficult.

I have right-sided weakness and shortness of breath. I'm doing anything I can *think* of to make breathing easier. It least I'm calm. Panicking would only distract me and interfere with that simple task. I put an icepack on my chest; I figure perhaps fatigue is causing my diaphragm to work harder. I don't know. I'm just grasping at straws. I even drank decaffeinated coffee this morning in case the caffeine was affecting my respiration and contributing to the nausea I've had for over two weeks. Well, by 2:00 p.m. I had an excruciating headache. I had a cup of coffee; abracadabra, *no* headache.

My dad and Rosalinda are coming over tonight. I have to be strong for those who love me. Anyway, I know God is watching me—this too shall pass.

My mom and I went to Scott's house the other day. His mom was also there. I have missed him so much. He makes me smile. He has trouble breathing, yet he is so strong. I think of his strength with every difficult breath I take.

Nancy called yesterday. I was so glad to hear from her. She has no idea how much I need my friends. She has no idea how much it meant to me that she called. I was too short of breath to tell her.

Friday, May 10, 1996

I have been sleeping poorly. I'm awakening throughout the night with terrible pain in my right ankle; I am also experiencing drop foot, so I drag that foot when I walk. I went to U of M yesterday to see a gastroenterologist about my nausea, as well as diarrhea, which I had all morning yesterday and the day before, with bloody stools. Because having to deal with MS is not enough? I weighed 116 pounds.

Tuesday, May 14, 1996

I had an upper endoscopy today that showed I have gastritis. Then I saw Dr. Sheremata, who assured me the MS will improve once this condition is treated.

After the docs, my mom and I went shopping for Rick's birthday present. We turned a tough morning into a meaningful fun day. At least I could focus on something other than my sore throat from the upper G.I. procedure, not to mention the memory of it. (When I was having it done, I was awake! I remember trying to remove the tube that was being shoved down my throat as the doctor and med-students watched. They were probably thinking I was just being difficult or something. I remember seeing the doctor after the procedure. I was *awake*; I think I was supposed to be sleepy! No worries, though—it's over.

Tuesday, May 21, 1996

My right hand is numb, and I still have drop foot in the right foot, but the *bad* news is that three nights ago my left side felt as though I had stuck it in a power outlet. Electric! This feeling has gotten progressively worse. Now, my left side feels like it's wearing an ankle weight and buckles. My left torso is also numb. I am cut in half from head to toe. I feel miserable, and I don't want to take Alpha tonight, but I will. My writing is troublesome because my right hand is numb.

On a lighter note, Rick gave me a surprise birthday party Saturday night for my thirtieth birthday! I was so surprised, I cried when I walked into a house full of friends who yelled, "Surprise!" I had a fun, not-thinking-of-MS, night. I'm sure it was a lot of work for Rick to pull this off. It is much appreciated.

Friday, May 23, 1996

It is my third day at JMH yet again. I feel worse today. I require total assistance to get out of bed to use the bathroom and the shower. I trust Dr. Sheremata, and I know he will make me better. Yes, that's a lot of pressure and faith I have in this doctor. I *trust* him.

I had a chest x-ray yesterday. I was also visited by PT and OT.

I'm hoping to be transferred to the suite with all the windows and space! I'm feeling I might be here for a while, and that's the room I was last in when I was a patient. The one who's there right now is being discharged today. She came to my room with another MS patient my first night here. They said the nurses on the floor had told them I was a nurse with MS, and since they had just been diagnosed, they had numerous questions. I enjoyed meeting them and having them to talk to as well.

Dr. Sheremata came in today and said that, because I started the Alpha when I was beginning to have an exacerbation, it had acted like Gamma, which makes the MS worse. I'm going to get an MRI again! Oh, well. "Keep smiling," he reminds me with a smile on his face. I comply.

May 28, 1996

I've been in the suite for a couple of days now. It's beautiful to look out at Miami. There is also a refrigerator, which allows me to put all the food everyone keeps bringing to me in hopes of making me eat. I don't have much of an appetite. I've gotten worse since I got here. On Saturday, Dr. Sheremata ordered a STAT MRI of the T-spine, which showed lesions at T3, T4, T7, and T8. I am so weak, the left side less than the right. My left arm is difficult to control, though; I drop everything. I can't walk. I can't do the wheelchair tour of the floor because my arms are weak. I can barely pump a hair-spray bottle to spray my long hair. I know this all sounds miserable, but I must keep my spirits up. It would be so easy to fall into this disease and let it take over when I am this weak. So I must be strong. I hate what it does to my family. I am fortunate to have them.

I love it that my room is decorated from my birthday with *happy thoughts!* There are balloons, cards, and pictures everywhere. I'm glad Scott called yesterday, too. I always like talking to him. I was also happy to see my dad and Rosalinda when they came by the last two nights. They were in Miami for something else this weekend.

Saturday, June 1, 1996

Rick is having such a hard time with this hospitalization. It's no wonder. He *is* a respiratory therapist with a wife who is having trouble breathing. He can't fix it. I get it. I had no idea until last night. He told me he is going to a counselor because I don't want to hear his doubts. I can't be his rock right now. I need him to be strong for me. I didn't know he was so stressed. He hadn't told me. I didn't want to know. I have enough on my mind. I hate that I can't control how this affects those who love me. I know I can only control how it affects me. I don't want to depend on them. In order for that to happen, I must do what I can to help myself. It reminds me of when you are in an airplane getting instructions for using the oxygen masks. You are told to put yours on first so you can help your child. I'm doing my best to take care of me, so others don't have to take care of me.

Anyway, the pulmonary physician told me to treat the MS, and that will treat the breathing problem. I'll take it as validation (it's not as if I have a choice).

Tuesday, June 4, 1996

I was so drugged last night from the Tegretol that has been put on hold right now to check my levels. I believe I am getting stronger, but the rubber-band feeling I have on my chest has not improved. I am so clumsy! I hate it. I know—*keep smiling*. There is talk about taking me to rehab, but I'll just stay here and go as an outpatient.

Tuesday, June 6, 1996

I coughed today! That means I took a deep breath. The rubber band around my chest is a little better, though worsens with exertion. I don't plan to go to rehab; I want to go home. I'm not ready yet, but I had a better day. I'm numb from head to toe tonight, but that's because I was active. I'm still clumsy. I spilled a cup of water on myself—gotta laugh! At least it was cold water instead of something hot like soup or coffee!

Saturday, June 7, 1996

I'm going home today! I lost my pen, so I'm writing in pencil. My writing is still sloppy. I'm still a klutz. That's probably how I lost my pen. My arms and hands are numb. So is my chest. It gets worse with exertion, but that's okay because I'm going home!

Wednesday, June 11, 1996

It's great to be home. I'm nauseated today. Rick has been wonderfully patient with me as I struggle with these conditions. I've been getting PT and OT. I get so SOB. I want to exercise more, but I fatigue easily. I must be patient and pace myself.

The numbness has lessened. My hands are still clumsy but improving. I start a new medication tomorrow for the rubber band around my chest because Tegretol makes my mouth dry, and the loss of appetite as well is something I can do without!

I am blessed with parents who love me. I *need* that right now. My mom is a saint. She doesn't look away from what I'm going through. She is always there for me. My dad has called me every day, which is unusual for him, but I'll take it!

Thursday, June 12, 1996

I'm disappointed in how Rick's handling me right now. No, this was *not* on our schedule. No, this is *not* how we planned our life for right now. This part of our life was totally out of the ball park! I'm doing my best with what I've got. I have faith in myself, my God, my ability to play with this very bad deck of cards I have been dealt. I would appreciate being treated like the wife he married, not a patient he doesn't want to care for. I would do that for him because love him. I believe you should treat others the way you want to be treated. That would include respect, not resentment. This is *not my fault.*

I'm doing better tonight, so he treats me differently. It's a relief, isn't it? I sure wish I could put MS on a shelf with no batteries for one day. Just one. That's all. Then I could literally catch my breath and be the old me. . . . Oh, yeah—I *am* the same me!

Sunday, June 15, 1996

My right arm is getting worse. It feels more like my left now. My hands and biceps feel stiff, numb, heavy, and clumsy. It is so hard to write.

Today was emotionally draining. Rick is having a hard time with this latest attack, feeling so out of control. He needs me to show that I'm fine. I need a break.

Actually, I'm walking now! Clumsy, but walking. I can feel my legs. Yippy! My numbness has lessened, too. The breathing problem is getting worse, but that is to be expected because I stopped the Tegretol due to nausea and switched to another anticonvulsive, Depakote.

When Dr. Sheremata discharged me last Saturday,

me gently told me my attack had had "a little pulmonary influence." I think he didn't want to scare me. Come on, what else can happen to frighten me? Not breathing is scary enough. I guess he was telling me enough. Sometimes I feel he is taking care of me with kid gloves. Thank you for taking care of me! I'll take it.

In 1992, I wrote in this journal about SOB with an exacerbation I was having while under Dr. Millan's care. Dr. Millan had said I had a lesion at C-2. Dr. Sheremata said this attack was with no new lesions, only reactive old ones. This SOB seems to be more likely due to a C-2 lesion than a T-3 or T-4. When I'm apneic, it's because my nerve isn't getting the message to breathe. Whatever. I just want to get this large animal off of my chest (that's what it feels like, anyway!).

So the Depakote is to treat the rubber band around my chest, which I'm not feeling as much as the breathing: When I talk, I get winded.

Derrick called me the other day. He tells me I'm beautiful even though he hasn't seen me in years. He reminds me that I'm strong and I'll get through this because I always do. I needed the positive comments! I'm choosing to forget the not-so-positive times with him. I must control what I can.

June 20, 1996

Scott called me yesterday. It's always nice to hear from him. He tells me sincerely, "You just have to get rid of the icks!" He means Derrick and Rick. He makes me laugh. I know he just wants to cheer me up. He is always successful! I wish he was here right now.

Friday, June 21, 1996

I'm lonely. Rick is at work (getting a much needed break from this situation). He continues to be there for me as I battle this disease. Theresa called today. I haven't talked to her since we were d/c'd from Jackson Memorial. It was great to laugh with her. We talked for a long time.

My breathing has been tough today. I'm getting spasms in my right calf and my bladder at night. I hope tomorrow is better. I'm still smiling and refuse to give into this disease.

Wednesday, July 3, 1996

I'm doing better today. My breathing has improved but I still can't yell. I guess some people might find that acceptable! That's funny, isn't it? Keeping a sense of humor is critical during these times.

The glands in my neck are swollen.

Thursday, July 25, 1996

My writing has improved, but on a very *serious* note. . .I'm losing my hair! It has been gracefully deposited all over our master bathroom floor. Fortunately, I'm blessed with loads of it, so it's not as noticeable to others.

Dr. Sheremata says it will probably take longer to get over this attack because these lesions are in a narrow part of the spinal cord, with decreased blood circulation. Fine, I think, I'm very patient. I can only walk short distances while dragging my right foot, no matter how gracefully I walk. This summer is so *hot*, too! I have trouble breathing, walking or talking! I'm so SOB right now. It's almost as if someone has a switch to turn my respirations on and off. I had a bad night because of right-side discomfort. It felt like burning electricity. I got up at 4:00 a.m. and got an ice pack, plus some Tylenol. Rick was so sweet; he helped me then held me until he had to go to work. I know he doesn't like to see me having trouble with anything! I want this to all go away, because I don't like to my loved ones having trouble with my struggles either!

9

NO, NO, NO!

Thursday, August 22, 1996

Scott's dad called me late last night to tell me that Scott passed away the night before.

As I get this news, I slowly sank to the floor and leaned against the wall, looking at the beautiful bracelet he had given me. I haven't taken it off, ever.

This news hurts so much. I haven't stopped crying. I barely slept last night just thinking of him. I feel almost betrayed, because he was in the hospital for the last three weeks and no one told me. I didn't get to say good-bye. I wasn't there to tell him, "Fight! You are stronger than this!" I didn't get to tell him how much he meant to me and how much I needed him. I didn't get to tell him what he would often tell me: "This disease sucks!" I would have reminded him how stubborn we are, and how I was always available to him no matter what, as he was to me.

He called me a month ago. It was almost as if he knew he was leaving, and he was calling to make sure I was getting better. This isn't how we *planned* it to be. We're supposed to fight this disease together. I feel abandoned, alone and scared. I would have liked to tell him how much he meant to me. I pray for strength to get through this impossible time. The picture of him sitting in the peacock chair in his home remains displayed on my dresser so I see it every day. I miss him terribly.

Rick has been supportive. He even brought me a dozen roses to cheer me up. I am grateful for his kindness during this very trying time. We are going to the funeral on Sunday. I don't know how I'll do seeing Scott in a casket, but I need to see for myself he is truly gone. I know he is no longer suffering, and he put up one hell of a fight. He was brave. Whenever I talked to him on the phone I told him I missed him. I wish I could tell him that now. He was my rock, my hero. When I was SOB, I'd remind myself of how strong Scott was, and that, if he could make it, so could I. Now he's gone. Now I have to be strong. This is hard. Please, God, give me that strength. (Important to have faith in a higher power—life is difficult on one's own.)

I'm still having trouble walking. I drag my right foot, which gets worse the more I walk. Rick brought home an orthopedic brace that seems to help my drop foot and ankle, but it's bulky and awkward. Nevertheless, I'm grateful to have it to use as needed. My SOB worsens with heat but overall has improved.

I'm glad Rick told my Dad and Rosalinda about Scott. It was nice to hear from them today. I had already told my mother. Samantha and Sue have been great, too. I am lucky to have people that care so much about me.

Sunday, August 25, 1996

Scott's funeral was today. I wanted to speak at the podium, but I couldn't stop crying. I had written a poem when I first heard of his passing, but I could barely speak. It was closed casket but I had to *see* him. His father let me do so after the service. He looked so peaceful wearing his baseball cap, just like always. I had to touch him to prove it was real, that he's gone. I miss him. His dad said, "You know he loved you."

I said, teary-eyed, "Yeah, I know. I loved him, too." I'd never actually said that to him, but I think he could see it in my face, my eyes, and my smile whenever I was with him. (Scott, I feel like there were so many things I didn't tell you, so many questions, so much unfinished business. How am I supposed to go on without you? Why didn't anyone tell me? Why didn't you say goodbye? When does this stop hurting?)

Dr. Sheremata was at the funeral as well. He reassures me the MS didn't kill Scott. But I'm not thinking about how my friend died, I'm thinking of my life without someone dear and close to my heart. Scott was such a gentleman. . . irreplaceable.

Monday, August 26, 1996

Scott's mom called me today. I was so glad to hear from her. I briefly talked to Scott's sister Wendy as well. I feel a little better after doing so. (We continue to exchange Christmas cards and occasionally speak on the telephone to this day. I feel like I'm talking to family in every conversation I have with Scott's family.) I plan to visit his mom with my mother in the near future. Scott's mom said she has some things to give me that were Scott's.

My MS is faring well through all this. I'm just tired. I'm still on the Depakote, so my hair continues to fall out; it's not noticeable to most. I'm dragging my right foot, so I can't wear heeled shoes because the ankle won't support me. No big deal. I fatigue easily.

I put everything that reminds me of Scott on my vanity— pictures, the talking bear, etc. I'll never take my bracelet off, ever.

Saturday, October 26, 1996

I can't find a pen, so I'm writing in pencil. I've been getting painful spasms in my right calf, and I'm SOB with exertion lately. Tomorrow we go to the Dolphins vs. Cowboys game! That should get my mind off this breathing issue!

Sunday, November 24, 1996

I lost the bracelet Scott gave me. I am devastated. I looked everywhere. I'm afraid it happened at the Dolphins game. I cherished it so much, and now it's gone. I called the stadium's lost-and-found, but I'm thinking, if someone found it, I'm sure they would keep it. I keep hearing Scott say, "Oh, Alys, don't worry about it." If he was alive, he wouldn't let it bother me. I think about him all the time.

I've been SOB today, but I also missed 1 dose of Depakote, and that's probably why. At times, I feel as though I'm choking or suffocating, strangled. It's very drastic and scary, but I remain calm and practice pursed-lip breathing as I would tell COPD patients to do when they were having trouble breathing. I hate this disease. I've gained a little weight. I'm 121 pounds now. Yuck! I'm comfortable at 118 to 120. Rick likes it—but I'll lose it ASAP (I hope!).

10

LIFE GOES ON

Monday, November 25, 1996

Thanksgiving is Thursday. Rick and I went to the mall today and he bought me a beautiful dress for the holidays. Now we *have* to go to Christmas parties!

Yeah! I weigh 120 pounds. I don't really care too much about my weight—I've never been heavy—I just like being in shape. I don't want to look too skinny!

I have a neighbor who also has MS. Sandy is a few years older than me. She is about my height, with short brown hair. She is an elementary school teacher. I used to see her occasionally riding her three-wheeled bike around the block. I spoke with her today. She said she has trouble breathing also. She also finds it difficult to yell or sing in her church choir. She continues to teach because it makes her happy. Her husband speaks of her fondly.

I've had a lot of trouble breathing today too, but I do my best to keep my mind off of it. I went shopping, to the gym, and cooked dinner. I know I overdid it, but I have no regrets. Only positive thoughts in this brain! I think I'm catching Rick's cold.

Friday, December 20, 1996

I brought home a kitty for Rick tonight to replace the cat he had that just died. He was attached to her, having had her for several years. Wow, was he surprised! She is so cute. She's six weeks old and has the same black-and-white coloring that Zubi had, and she is such a fur ball! I got her at the wildlife refuge next to the animal shelter. I got lucky, because a volunteer at the shelter took me over there, and they gave her to me for free! They'd found these kittens alone in the wild and rescued them. She is perfect. She is precious. Rick gives her the name Glowi, after his mother's name, Gloria, who passed away recently.

Thursday, February 6, 1997

The holidays were wonderful, as always. We celebrated *Noche Buena* at our house. I enjoy cooking the *lechon* for dinner. I'm trying to adjust the recipe that my mom gave me to create my own. Rick gave me a lovely bracelet to wear in place of the one I lost. I love it. I love that he acknowledges how much it meant to me. It was probably difficult for him to watch me wearing a bracelet given to me by another man.

This year has already started to challenge our strength and faith. Our next-door neighbor, Tara, the one who called me at Jackson about the progress of our pool construction, has passed away. She was only forty-five. She died of an aneurysm. Dave, her husband, is having a hard time, as expected. I suspect this was not his vision of growing old together. I recall her telling me how they were going to travel once the two girls were grown. If you don't do it when you're thinking about it, it won't get done.

We can only reassure him that we are here for him and his daughters. Also, my Uncle Eddie has just been diagnosed with colon cancer. He is scheduled for a colon resection next week. I pray they are able to remove all the cancer. I volunteered to work at his store recently, and I really enjoyed it because I was around people. I enjoy nursing for that reason, among others. The register was easy to operate because I'd worked at Jordan Marsh. For some reason, I found the Lotto machine troublesome, though. (I learned why later; it wasn't MS.) I don't know if it's worth the energy I expend to volunteer, but he is my uncle, and I love him, so I will help with what I can.

I stopped taking the Alferon. I feel great today! I probably feel good because it made me fatigued, I don't know. It was probably not the wisest thing to do, but

I'll pay for it later. I just wanted to feel like me again.

Now we are looking at a trip to Hawaii! I pray I feel good in May. We are going to Orlando this weekend. We are celebrators. We have to return to where Rick proposed to me and mark the day as one to celebrate! I'm looking forward to getting away, and so is he.

Today is Easter Sunday. It's 3:40 p.m. I'm sitting outside, by the pool, like a fool, because I can barely breathe. It is *so hot!* I just had to get out of the house, though. I've had a lot of trouble breathing lately, especially with activity but also without. I'm seeing Dr. Ludwig, who also has me as an outpatient in pulmonary rehab at Palms West Hospital (anything but drugs!). I'm so happy not being on meds! I'm only taking Valium for spasms. I hope to get this respiratory problem under control. I'm so glad my hair is growing back too since I stopped the Depakote. (But that's what hats and wigs are for, dummy.) I'm not so depressed since I stopped the Alpha, too! I'm making my own rules in an attempt to control this uncontrollable situation.

Friday, April 4, 1997

I've stayed home to rest for the past three days. I speak in barely a whisper. My lips get numb from chewing gum! I just need to rest, no meds. I mean, I need to rest *and* take meds, but I'm not ready to accept that yet.

It is so hard to breathe. Walking from room to room

is such an effort. I must keep my spirits up. I wish Scott was here. He would have gotten my mind out of this rut.

Tuesday, May 27, 1997

Tomorrow we leave for Hawaii at 7:00 a.m.! I'm feeling I can handle this. I purchased a cool purple wheelchair that folds up like a stroller and weighs less than twenty pounds. I'm tired. Aloha!

Wednesday, July 2, 1997

Hawaii was *wow!* We had a fantastic time. I felt fairly well. It was a long flight but tolerable. Having the wheelchair was a blessing, but I walked most of the time. I mean, come on, it's *Hawaii*; I really wanted to experience it *up!* You know, *standing up!* We got leis when we came off the plane, and from then on, we made the most of every moment. In Honolulu we did everything we could think of that was Hawaiian, then flew to Maui and stayed for a few days, then flew to the Big Island to stay for a few days, then flew to Kaui for a few more days. We went to luaus on each of the islands, shows, shopping, tours, and we ate delicious food at various restaurants. I kept being asked if I was an island girl! It must be my long hair or something. My favorite island was the Big Island of Hawaii. It had volcanoes, beautiful black sand beaches, and waterfalls. All the islands were beautiful, though. I could go back easily!

Poor Rick fell on some lava rocks while taking a picture on one of our tours in Maui, and we had to go to the clinic and get antibiotics, so no snorkeling for us! If he can't, I won't! After that, his leg turned red and swollen and infected. He's better now.

I've been nauseated and vomited after dinner Saturday night. I've lost some weight and don't have much of an appetite. I went to Dr. Neimark (GI), who ordered Prilosec and Karafate for that. Tomorrow, I go to Dr. Sheremata because my pharmacist told me Sheremata wanted to see me. Uh, oh—I haven't told him I discontinued the Alferon. I think Dr. Ludwig mentioned it to him, though. I feel okay MS-wise. I went to the gym today and had a good workout. My muscles are strong, left more than right. I drag my right foot after short distances and fatigue easily. I'm tired. I haven't been sleeping well.

Monday, July 14, 1997

Dr. Sheremata's visit went well. He wants MRIs done again, so I'm scheduled for later this month.

We leave for Toronto on Thursday for six days. We fly into Buffalo, New York, then drive to the Canadian side of Niagara Falls, and then to Toronto for three nights. I'm wiped out just thinking about it! I am so nauseated that flying in a plane doesn't sound appealing right now. The MS is steady, no ups and downs of symptoms. (I did well on this trip. We enjoyed the magnificent experience of the Falls in Canada, followed by many tourist stops, and did more touring in Toronto, followed by going to see *The Phantom of the Opera,* which was a terrific show, while we were there.

I saw Nancy at the gym today. She's currently going through tough times of her own. I hope things work out for her. I'm glad she called me tonight.

As for the MS, I don't notice any new symptoms, I just tire easily. Still no meds—I'm only taking Valium at bedtime.

Thursday, October 23, 1997

I'm *so* SOB today. I feel as if an elephant is standing on my chest. I guess I just overdid it again when we went to Key West this past week end. We had a blast! We stayed at Ocean Key House, right on Duval Street. On Friday and Saturday night they had a Latin band playing music to salsa to. I danced lots! We had so much fun on Duval Street, where we walked everywhere. Walking a lot is never good for my MS. I'm dragging my right foot almost always now. I notice how easily I fatigue lately.

It just dawned on me the other day that all those patients with MS at Jackson were on ventilators. I don't want to believe it's the same illness I have, but when I can't breathe, I'm struck with that possibility. Perhaps there is variation in how MS affects different patients. Yes, that thought works for me. God help me. Thus, I continue to make the most of each day, each moment. I know I have many to look forward to. I continue to have right-sided weakness, though. I mostly notice it when I'm playing with Glowi or working out. I tires easily. Driving is also fatiguing; so is writing. I'm done now.

Monday, November 3, 1997

I haven't been feeling too great these past few days. Thursday my left side felt different than my right, as if I had been cut in half. The left side felt tingly; I could have been wearing leather pants on that side. I'm still SOB, like a light switch turning on or off. Today, the left side of my face also feels different. That's not good. I have an appointment to see Dr. Sheremata on November 18.

On the good side of the past week, I saw my long-time friend Ismara! I haven't seen her in over ten years! She came over and we talked a lot. She has always been a good friend. She has been going through tough times herself. I pray for good times in the future for her.

Thursday, November 6, 1997

So much for November 18. Tonight is my second night at Jackson Memorial. I was admitted yesterday after seeing Dr. Sheremata. I am so sleepy. I was awakened throughout the night. Rick stayed with me on a small bed. I didn't get my ACTH until after 1:30 a.m. Today was exhausting, and I can't wait to get a good night's sleep. I am *sooo* SOB and *sooo* fatigued. I must have been examined by five or six different people. *No med students to touch pt.*—that's the order Dr. Sheremata is giving for me. He was quite upset. I'm looking forward to resting tonight.

November 7, 1997

I slept better last night. I'm speaking with a louder voice (yes!). Last night Dr. Sheremata spoke to me about long- term treatment. He mentioned T-cells. He didn't say much more except that, with my genetic makeup in relation to MS, I basically need some form of treatment. He said we will discuss it further in the future.

Saturday, November 8, 1997

H-E-L-P me breathe. . . .

I have been struggling to all day. My mom and her mother were here this morning. I am so sleepy. Dr. Sheremata came in this evening. I really need a good night's sleep. It's 8:oo p.m., and I'll get my medicine early tonight. Then it's good night!

Sunday, November 9, 1997

It's evening, so Rick should be here soon. He's staying here tonight. I miss him; I haven't seen him in two days. It's been a bad breathing day. I go for MRI and PFTs tomorrow, and that's going to wipe me out. I feel so weak; everything requires so much effort. If any nurse wakes me up tonight, I think Rick is going to kill them! (Just kidding, of course.)

Saturday, November 15, 1997

My mom spent the day here yesterday and the day before. We actually had a great time. We laughed so much together. She keeps my spirits up and makes me smile and laugh. We made many friends between patients, visitors, and even staff. That makes it that much easier to be here.

Tuesday, November 18, 1997

I'm feeling much stronger today. Sheremata says I'm staying the full twenty-one-day course. Last night he had a long talk with me concerning the course of the MS and its effect on me. He bluntly said I have large bites taken from my spinal cord. He said they are permanent and will not return. He told me I need to consider long-term treatment. He continues to encourage the Alferon; he tells me I did poorly on it because I started it during an exacerbation, but that he has five hundred patients on it, and that they haven't had an exacerbation for up to five years.

I spoke to a nurse here about this medication. She told me she doesn't see Alpha patients anymore—it keeps them out of the hospital, she said. I don't have to decide now. Sheremata has encouraged me to take my time and think about it.

Saturday, November 22, 1997

Today was a good day! I had a good breathing day! I still get SOB with exertion but I'm doing *much* better. Mom spent the day with me. We had fun.

Dr. Sheremata was here this morning. I told him my decision to retry the Alpha. He says I will do better this time, that I have to be at my optimum to begin it. I am more mentally willing to accept this treatment faced with the facts of my illness. Besides, he said this treatment has the least number of side effects, and I'm already familiar with them. I have to believe it will work for me. It has to. He says three exacerbations in one year is a big red flag.

Sunday, November 23, 1997

Papi was just here. He came with the whole family. I was so glad to see them. Today was another good day. I just keep getting better and better. Dr. Sheremata was here this morning and said I can go home tomorrow! He says, if I crash after receiving ACTH (and I do), to wait four days to start the Alpha. I'm psyched about it this time. I want to do well on it. I really want it to work for me. I really *need* it to work for me. I can't wait to go home!

November 24, 1997

I went straight to bed at 7:00 p.m. I woke up in the morning from a nightmare. I dreamt I was going to go into my pool but went to the neighbor's house instead.

I saw him get out of his pool dressed in a wet suit, as though he was preparing to go scuba diving. When I looked at his face, he had on a mask connected to an oxygen tank. As I reached out to it, he said, "No. This is mine." He continued, "Your doctor says you have to use your muscles to breathe." I stared at him with my face white and lips blue, wishing I could use his tank. I felt like I was drowning all night. I slept with the head of the bed up to help with breathing.

I tell everyone I'm fine, though, because I am. I just have to pace myself. I'm tired, so today I thought I would take it easy. Yeah, right. I woke up this morning, took a shower, then off to OT at 9:30 a.m. Then, after lying down for half an hour, I was taken to PT. I finally rested all afternoon in bed.

Saturday, November 29, 1997

It's nice to be home! I'm feeling way better by just being here. We went to my sister's house for Thanksgiving dinner. We stayed there for about an hour. That was my first day back home. I wasn't feeling well, but I had to go. After all, it was Thanksgiving Day, and I wasn't in the hospital, so I just had to go! Getting dressed, traveling, and talking wiped me out. My chest was sore and tired that night. I didn't sleep all night because I couldn't lie down, because I couldn't breathe. I just wanted to cry, but I couldn't breathe so I couldn't do that either!

Tuesday, December 2, 1997

Last night Rick injected my first shot of Alpha. He does the hips for me as I rotate sites. It didn't hurt at all. At about 3:30 a.m. the chills started along with the body aches. Today I was miserable with flu like symptoms (headache, low grade temp., chills, nausea.)

Mom came over tonight. We watched a movie. It was really good. Mom knows how to keep my mind off of my illness. Just spending time with her keeps my mind off of the illness! She is a joy.

Thursday, December 4, 1997

I slept soundly last night. Of course, I didn't get a shot. Those come every *other* night. So last night was restful, except that I still had the delight of experiencing side effects, just not so drastic. Unfortunately, the day that followed was reminiscent of the previous one. Still, as I exhibit the SOB, weak and shaky limbs, numb lips, and numb right hand and both feet, I convince myself of the importance of a positive attitude. That night, I got my second shot, followed by a night with decreased side effects, just sweats, but the breathing caused my night to be not so restful. I slept sitting straight up from 10:00 p.m. to 1:00 a.m. I tried to lie on my side, but I couldn't breathe when I did. So I just sat there and prayed. I had only positive thoughts, convincing myself how God wouldn't give me something I wasn't capable of handling. I prayed, "God, I just want to lie down and sleep like a normal person, just for a little while." It's been so long since I could sleep lying on my back. I put this disease in God's hands and told him that I knew he would not abandon me. Thy will be done. I prayed for him to give me strength to handle this challenging time. I thanked Him for bringing me closer to him through my suffering, and to give me strength until then. I prayed for him to stay with me until then. I was awake until 4:00 a.m., when at last I felt such peace and comfort. I was drawn down to my mattress. I was either totally exhausted, or God had answered my prayers! I believe that, no matter what the future brings, I will be strong; I will be capable of dealing with my life, because it's *my* life. I will control that which I can. I continue to learn how much power my mind has on my body!

Seeing how this is up to me, the following day, I proceeded with RT, PT, and OT, and wrote out my bills (because they come regardless of how you feel). Go! Go! Go! Oh, I did manage a short nap; I paced myself today. I took a shower after the nap, which was tiring because I was alone, but I like to take care of myself. It was my first day alone, because Rick went to work, but I look forward to being independent. I'm getting a routine. I pace myself at *my* discretion. I think of what I'm going to do and how to do it using the least amount of energy expended. This is such a challenge, but I like challenges! I'm going to be all right. I keep smiling as I sit here with these side effects and SOB.

Sunday, December 14, 1997

Right now, it's cool outside but wet. Once the rain stops, it should be cool, but right now I feel like I'm drowning. Rick opened the windows today because it was cool, but if I could scream right now, I would. I could feel the humidity in an instant. I don't care if it's freezing outside to others; that shuts me down immediately. Rick keeps asking me why I'm having so much trouble breathing. What he doesn't realize is that I *usually* have trouble breathing, I just don't show it! I would tell him, but I struggle to breathe. I'm much more active when he's home. I look forward to activity; I must pace myself to make it possible to do more than nothing.

Thursday, December 25, 1997

Last night we had our traditional Christmas Eve dinner as we have for the past four years. I'm tired. We haven't opened our gifts to each other yet because Rick went to work. It's a quiet Christmas day. I'll take it— I'm tired after last night!

January 13, 1998

I don't feel well today. I'm like the day I went into the hospital, quite winded, and my lips, tongue, and feet are numb. I'm a soft talker, but everything is such an effort for me to do. I'm scared. I was feeling better for a while. I've been increasing my activity looking for a wall unit for our TV. That is something I can do because I enjoy getting out of the house.

New Year's Eve, Rick and I went out to dinner. I had a tiny sip of champagne. I haven't had any liquor in a long time, but it was New Year's Eve! Anyway, I'm trying to figure out why the MS is acting up. I may have a cold. I've been coughing the past few days. At least I felt better for the holidays. Rick got me beautiful diamond earrings. I wear them every day. He didn't have to buy me such an extravagant gift; he never listens. I'm hoping to feel better by taking it easy.

Thursday, April 30, 1998

Talk about stress, its 12:30 a.m., and I can't sleep. I haven't slept well for three nights. My car has been giving me trouble, too. I don't want to put money into it, because I really need an automatic. I get so fatigued and clumsy driving a manual. I finally found what I want, a small SUV. It's easy to get in and out of, and it's automatic. I have no *money*, but I'll find a way. I have to.

May 13, 1998

I love my new truck! It's easy to get into, and driving is a breeze. No more stick shift. I sure do miss my Rx-7, but it's time for a change.

June 21, 1998

It's been quite a month. For Rick's fortieth birthday, I gave him a surprise B-day party. He was *truly* surprised. That weekend we went to Orlando to celebrate our birthday, and we both ended up getting sick! He got food poisoning, and I got a bladder infection. I had antibiotics delivered to our hotel. We drove home the next day—our birthday!

The following weekend we went to Cancun for our fifth wedding anniversary, and I got sick—*again*. This time the bladder infection turned into pyelonephritis. I had severe pain of my lower back and a lot of blood when urinating. I couldn't wait to get home!

I ended up going straight to WRMC and was admitted for six days. Not only was I given antibiotics, but they had to treat me for dehydration, anemia, and thyroid disease (hypothyroid)! There is a lump in my neck, which I had biopsied. What next?

January 20, 1999

I have another urinary tract infection. Dr. Sheremata says he has lost a lot of kidneys! I never thought *I* would have to worry about losing one! He says it's a common complication of MS. Wonderful.

I have to get through this, because, otherwise, I've been feeling fairly well (MS-wise).

We had a fun New Year's Eve at Bongos Restaurant, featuring Latin bands and Desi Arnaz, plus delicious food and fireworks!

My thyroid is finally under control; thus the reason for the difficulty with the lottery machine at my uncle's store: It was difficult to push the correct buttons. My hair is growing back —curly, but that's not a bad thing. I've been feeling extremely well! I even cooked dinner for *Noche Buena!*

11

AND ON

March 13, 1999

It's been a fairly active week. On Monday, I received a call from Dr. Sheremata. He asked me how I'm doing on the Alferon (side effects, etc.), and also how I'm doing with MS. I told him, "I'm fine, except for these dreaded UTIs!"

He said to me, "When did you plan to see me?"

Next thing I knew, I was in his office two days later. He'd also said, "No Cipro!" Many doctors don't know that Cipro causes the Interferon not to work. Oops, I think, I was *on* it for ten days! Sheremata also said that, because the thyroid is part of the immune system and Alpha also affects the immune system, it could have some effect on the thyroid. I miss Scott. I think about him when I want to talk about these MS complications, or when I just want to talk. I think about him all the time.

Tomorrow, Rick and I go to Orlando to celebrate our engagement anniversary. We go every year. It's nice to have that to look forward to. Oh—I weigh 111 pounds, a skinny size 1! Thank God for those Latin hips to give me some shape!

Saturday, March 21, 1999

I was given samples of Detrol to try instead of Valium for bladder spasms. Hopefully, my nights will be undisturbed by feeling like I have to go to the restroom!

I was pleasantly surprised by a visit from my dear friend Ismara. It's always good to see her. Apparently, she recently visited Cuba! That's where we differ. Growing up, we would tell strangers we were twins! We were best friends with the same haircut, we both have Chinese grandfathers, and we even have the same freckle on the same hand! I, however, I have never been to Cuba. I want to hear all about it.

Friday, November 5, 1999

I went to my first class last night for the Crisis Line. This is perfect for me! I'm going to answer calls as a volunteer. First, I must complete a course, and that started last night. Sunday is orientation. But what I wanted to write about is how perfect this is for me. It's why I became a nurse, to help those whom I can. I'm grateful that I can make a difference in someone's life, and that MS is not preventing me from doing it. I'm even more grateful that

I *want* to do it! A year ago, I had no desire to do anything because of MS and medications, not to mention the resulting depression and fatigue. I have been feeling more like myself and that I could attempt something without fearing an MS hospitalization. It has been close to two years since I've been in the hospital with an exacerbation. I've had attacks, but not so severe that I needed hospitalization. I can also see my walking is worsening, and my balance as well, but these symptoms have been more chronic than acute, so I have to adjust to them. It's a bother, but I believe I can do it. I mean, it is *more* than a bother, but I must believe in myself and have faith that I can get through it. I twisted my ankle last night when I got home. *Ouch!* I was merely walking in the living room, but my right side is the weaker right now, and it was the end of the day, so it was even weaker and more fatigued. I put ice on it, which seemed to help—it's just sore.

Anyway, I look forward to making a difference in someone's life, be it big or small, it doesn't matter—I simply want to give my existence meaning and my life purpose. I refuse to let MS get the better of me, so I keep fighting it with all my strength, a smile on my face and God in my heart.

Friday, November 18, 1999

I can't believe I fell. I'd needed a mental break, so I'd gone to the Boynton Mall to look around. It had been a stressful week.

I was strolling happily when, before I knew it, the hard floor was too close to my face! My feet had gone numb, but I'd thought that, if I just kept them moving and made believe I was walking, I'd be alright. Granted I wasn't using any support, not even a cane. So I fell, hard, on my good right knee.

No one would help me. They probably assumed I was drunk.

I finally got the attention of a girl working in the store in front of which I had fallen. I explained, "I have MS, and that's why I fell." As I was doing so, a kindly older couple approached me and asked if they could help in any way. They allowed me to lean on the gentleman's shoulder and assisted me to my truck.

I kept smiling and thanking them, assuring them repeatedly that I was fine.

As soon as I was in my truck, though, I covered my face with the palms of my hands as I scrunched forward towards the steering wheel and just cried and cried. My knee hurt; *I* hurt. I couldn't believe it, couldn't *believe* I had fallen like that. I usually catch myself, but there had been nothing there to grab onto.

I got home and iced my knee the rest of the day. I even made dinner—standing like an idiot, cooking, I'm freakin' nuts! Who did I think I was? I hadn't wanted to cook the *next* day because I had class for the crisis line at 6:00 p.m.

That night was hell. My knee hurt so badly I couldn't put weight on it by morning. Fortunately, Rick was home. He took me to the WRMC emergency room. They gave me a brace once my knee was x-rayed. They also gave me pain meds.

Wonderful.

If it's not better in one week, I need to be seen by an orthopedist. I ended up missing the class at Crisis Line, but they assured me it wouldn't be a problem.

This week was stressful because we went to Orlando Saturday and Sunday; I had to take my mom to get a procedure done on Monday. She was sick on Tuesday, so I took her to the doctor that morning. Then I fell on Wednesday. I don't want her or Rick to worry about me. She has to take care of herself.

I hate this disease.

November 27, 1999

It hurts! My knee hurts more today than yesterday. I've behaved about my physical activity, limiting what I do as much as possible. God, this is so painful!

Monday, November 29, 1999

I go to Dr. Rondon (an orthopedist) tomorrow. The MS is not cooperating with my injury right now! My lips are so numb, I'm speaking with a slur at times. I'm tired—it was a busy weekend. Rick was off, so we did tons of shopping!

January 27, 2000

I hate the way I feel today. I am extremely sleepy because my bladder is preventing me from sleeping soundly. I'm in the bathroom every hour. I would welcome a solid eight-hour sleep without interruption! When I do get up, I'm disappointed with the very minimal results. I can barely urinate (slow, weak stream). That's not bothering me as much as my *speech*, though, which is slow and slurred. I sound like I have MS, and I hate it. It's hard to stay optimistic when I feel so bad.

My left knee hurts. I hit it last night one of the many times I got out of bed to use the bathroom. Since falling in the mall on my right knee, I've learned that I tore my left lateral collateral ligament. That was back in November, and it continues to hurt, especially if I bend it. I can't bend it at all since I fell. That injury has not stopped bothering me to this day. I still have trouble bending this knee. Dr. Rondon drained quite a bit of fluid from it last month, but it remains swollen.

I went to see Dr. Sheremata this week. It has been about a year since I saw him. The speech problem is new for me. I'm also having balance issues. So, I might as well say I'm a slurring, weeble-wobble toy. He says I am stable, but he wants to be sure by getting MRIs. He said, "I never make assumptions."

Thursday, February 1, 2000

I went to see Dr. Rondon yesterday. He ordered a different brace and ugly crutches for me because I keep falling down and re-injuring my knee. I will go tomorrow; I'm drained of energy today. I also need to get my blood drawn for Dr. Sheremata to see if I might be able to decrease my dosage of Alferon. It may be causing anemia and leading to my feeling tired.

Thursday, February 3, 2000

I just got off the phone with Dr. Sheremata, who gave me the results of yesterday's blood test. He also told me to stop the Alferon for two to three weeks, and then to restart it at every three days. I have an appointment to see him on the 25th. I told him about my difficulty breathing. He said everything is flaring up, but that I will be okay. I said, "I know."

Well, I do! Really, I know. It's kind of hard to believe, but, I know. I mean, I really believe I *will* be okay. I don't know what is in store for me in the future, but I am confident I will handle it to the best of my ability. I know. I keep smiling. Heck, I've made it this far! I can laugh, or I can cry. I hope I feel better with the adjustment of the medication. Time will tell.

Also, I'm having trouble being able to tell someone about my difficulty breathing. I hesitate to tell my husband because he wants to *correct* the problem (bi-pap machine, inhalers, etc.). Bless him for that. I tell my doctor because I should. I don't have expectations. I just want to be able to tell someone and voice my frustrations about it. It really is an inconvenience! I mostly just need to be validated. I would welcome someone to tell me, "That sucks!" Oh, yeah—that someone would be Scott.

I have to mention also that Ismara sent me a beautiful letter yesterday. It included stories about the fun times we used to have when we were young. It put a smile on my face. I appreciate the thoughtfulness it required to write it for me. She has always been a true friend.

Tuesday, February 8, 2000

My speech is much improved, as is my energy level. What a difference! Last week, after my morning coffee, I was still unaffected by the caffeine. Today, I notice the increased energy. Short lived, but so? My left lip, ankle, and knee are numb. The swelling persists at the knee. I'm icing it right now. I just exercised it gently and minimally. Tomorrow I get fitted for a new brace because I keep injuring it. Hopefully, it will help, so I won't continue to hurt my knee by accidentally falling as I walk! I seem to keep re-injuring it that way, or by bumping it. My coordination stinks!

Wednesday, February 16, 2000

I got my Bledsoe brace two days ago. It looks like a robot leg. It covers my whole leg. Hopefully, my knee will heal with the brace to keep me from injuring it. My speech remains the same. I thought it had improved but actually it actually alternates from normal to impaired, in a manner similar to that of other MS symptoms. I feel all right, but I'm not surprised; whenever I stop the Interferon, I seem to feel better. I have increased energy, which leads to feeling more like me. I still have symptoms such as dizziness, coordination problems, and, most bothersome, cognitive ones, along with memory alterations. I've had the last two before, before but they are more pronounced now. What I do notice is that, no matter what hell I am confronted with concerning MS, it's much easier to handle when I'm not depressed.

We had a nice Valentine's Day. We went to dinner and Rick got me a dozen roses—sweet.

Saturday, February 26, 2000

I started the Alferon again last night. My night was quite unpleasant. I experienced a repeat of flu-like symptoms that included sweats, chills, and headache. Even worse, I kept Rick up, too. I don't want to share these troublesome times with *anyone*. My knee hurts terribly today.

My MRIs don't show any new lesions. That's what Dr. Sheremata told me yesterday when I went to his office. "I'm not surprised," he continued. "I have not seen new lesions with patients treated with Alpha for MS." Hallelujah. He did seem a bit concerned about my speech but said it should resolve itself in approximately six months without further treatment. I'm not about to treat this complication with anticonvulsive drugs! I'll just wait. Hopefully, it will improve in its own with the Alpha. He also recommended a physician for my knee. I think I'll just stay with my local doctor. I can only deal with so much right now. I appeared pinker to him than I was the last time he saw me on the 25th. My speech is about the same with slurring, dragging my words. I sound like I have MS. I sound like Scott. I miss my friend so much. We were supposed to go through this disease together.

While in the waiting room for two hours to see Dr. Sheremata, I spoke with another patient who also had experienced speech problems with MS. She told me her name was Trisha, and that she was from West Palm Beach. Turned out she was there as a result of my recommendation when I spoke to her two years ago! What a coincidence. I have never met her. I only spoke to her by phone! As a result of our conversation, she discontinued seeing her neurologist, whom she was unhappy with, and started seeing Dr. Sheremata. She seemed content with her decision.

I've had a headache for the past two days, since I restarted Alpha. I have been popping Tylenol like crazy. I continue wearing the long brace on my leg. I have yet to bend my left knee completely. I haven't been able to totally bend it since November. I've felt dizzy but, otherwise, I have energy, which I love. I've also been getting compliments on my hair! I guess it finally looks healthy again after two years of Alpha.

Ismara came over yesterday with her mother. It was like being visited by family. I hadn't seen her mother in *years*. It's been about a year since I saw Ismara. She has always been a true friend.

Thursday, March 23, 2000

I hate the way I feel today. I have no energy. Yesterday, I went in the pool, and it felt great. I'm hoping to get in it today. I needed to get out of the house yesterday, so I went to Target briefly, but I was dizzy and SOB, which made that a short trip. I am careful.

My mom's mom (Abuela Olga) is returning to Cuba on Saturday. She misses her friends and neighbors. That just shows me how vital it is to have others to share life with. She likes it here in America but is willing to return to the place she has known as home for all these years. My mom works during the day. So Abuela has been home alone.

My energy, yesterday, was better, which probably means I did too much! I've been exercising.

Wednesday, March 29, 2000

I feel yucky today—heavy, weak, SOB, and dizzy. I have no energy. I've been exercising in the pool. Hopefully, that is helping my knee, which still hurts.

Thursday, March 30, 2000

I feel worse today than yesterday. My night was horrible. Between the achy pain in my legs and the struggle to breathe, I was eager for the morning to arrive. I have heavy and weak extremities to add to my misery. My headache doesn't seem to lessen, either. It remains throughout the day. I was up throughout the night, constantly thinking I needed to use the bathroom. I continue to speak oddly. I just want to curl up in a dark corner until I get better. I hate how I feel.

Tuesday, April 18, 2000

I hate the way I feel today. I don't want to see or talk to anybody. I have no energy. I'm lonely and depressed. I don't understand why I feel this way. I haven't had Alferon for twelve days. I thought I would feel great by now. *Wrong-o.* I feel worse.

On Sunday, Rick and I went his father's house to see him. We took him shopping for clothes for him for our vacation to Las Vegas next month. He will be going with us, as well as my mother. Rick and I are celebrating our anniversary. We thought they could use a vacation. I hope I don't feel like this!

12

I TRIP
AND WE TAKE TRIPS

June 13, 2000 Tuesday

I feel so tired. I'm not sleepy, just devoid of energy. We went to Las Vegas for our anniversary. Rick's dad and my mom went as well. We stayed at the Venetian. We had three rooms—Dad Capozzi had his, my mom had hers, and ours was between them. Fortunately we were all on the same floor! We have been at this hotel before, so we knew our parents would like it as well. We enjoyed having them there. They would run off and do various things together while Rick and I did ours. We all enjoyed ourselves. We went to the Grand Canyon on our anniversary day. That same evening, Rick and I had dinner at the Eiffel Tower in the Paris casino. It was delicious! When we got back to our room, I was so surprised—Rick had strewn rose petals from the doorway to our bed! It was so romantic.

I almost fell down the escalator at Caesar's Palace the same day. We went there with Mom and Dad. Luckily, Rick held me, so I wouldn't tumble down. I hurt my feet, but it could have been much worse. These are the times when it's nice to have our parents there to comfort us! Rick bought me a pretty dress to wear to dinner that night. He said it would make me feel better. I told him I didn't need to get it, but he wanted to do something. I think that near-catastrophe really scared him. It scared me, too! My feet are scratched and bruised, but it could have been worse. It could have been *me* at the bottom of the escalator instead of my cane and shoes! It's also humorous how many security personnel appeared out of nowhere to make sure I was okay. It *is* a casino, so I'm sure someone is watching me.

I'm having more trouble with my balance and coordination. Before we left for Vegas, I caught my right hand in the car door, but I didn't realize it right away (delayed reaction). When I saw my hand in the door, I suddenly felt the terrible pain; I screamed and took it out. I cried so hard. It was very painful. Now I have an ugly black thumbnail, which is also very numb. I'm a mess from head to toe. Did I mention I also have a bladder infection? I hope to feel better soon. After all, next month we are going to New York City to see

Broadway shows and take some tours. We're only going for three nights, which is plenty. I'm sure we will enjoy ourselves.

Sunday, June 17, 2000

I'm finding it more and more difficult to breathe. I immediately find myself winded with the simplest activity. For example, *breathing* or *walking,* even *talking!* My speech is awkward, but I continue to smile. I know it could be so much worse, I guess. I'm doing my best to live with what I've got right now. That would be: hair on my head, a smile on my face, and. . .I'm having trouble thinking of a third. Oh! And a roof over my head! It *is* something, after all! Come on, how much worse it would be if I was this ill and homeless? I must keep a sense of humor to be successful at this horrid fight.

My knee has improved. I haven't worn a brace for a few weeks. I still am unable to bend it completely.

Wednesday, June 21, 2000

I slept well last night, I think; at least I feel rested. This morning I took my last antibiotic for the bladder infection I had. I'm hoping to feel better from not being on antibiotics.

Friday, June 23, 2000

Struggling to breathe, I was awakened this morning. I'm finding it difficult to breathe while lying flat on my back. I am scheduled to see Dr. Sheremata this afternoon at 1:00 p.m. I'm not very worried about the breath-ing. It's just bothersome. It's hard to do anything when you can't breathe! My legs, thighs, and feet are numb, but I'm still walking!

Thursday, June 30, 2000

I'm having quite rough time breathing. My legs don't work as well as they used to, but I still walk short distances before the weakness, in my legs or the SOB, starts acting up. I continually give myself pep talks to help me manage this illness. My visit with Dr. Sheremata didn't go as well as I was anticipating. I didn't care for the way I felt when I left. You know, he usually says something to make me *feel* better. When I asked, "Will the breathing get better? or "Do you think it's adjusting the dose of Alferon that flared up the breathing symptom?" he said, "No." I just wanted to hear "It will eventually improve" or something else encouraging. Instead he just kept recommending *other* doctors for different symptoms—like the ENT for my speech problem, the pulmonary doctor for the respiratory problem, etc. I don't want to see any more doctors if they aren't going to cure me. This is getting old. He wouldn't really answer my questions, and the worst part was the "fellow" doctor who did my exam. He was reminiscent of seeing another doctor rather than solely seeing Dr. Sheremata, as I have in the past. This fellow wasn't warm and friendly, which is what I'm used to. I don't want to go back to see Dr. Sheremata if it means I have to be seen by this other guy. He wasn't awful, merely depressing. He told me I was lucky to be walking. He proceeded to tell me I should see an EMT because I'm thirty-four years old, so I shouldn't be talking this way. Dr. Sheremata had told me it would improve, *and it did.* I have been speaking normally to this day. The guy needs instruction on bedside manners! I am aware of my crappy MRIs, I know my condition may not be as expected, but don't you know I refuse to let MS *win* this fight? So I continue to move what I can, so this body doesn't forget! I can't give up, I just can't. I won't.

About volunteering at the Crisis Line, it's not going to happen. My speech is causing this plan to be altered. So, everything happens for a reason.

Saturday, July 30, 2000

My energy is so short-lived. It's 10:30 a.m. I'm wiped out. I'm clumsy and dragging my legs after a short walk in the house. I'll admit I've done a few things this morning. I washed Zubi (which includes brushing, combing, blow-drying, and putting his fur up in a ponytail to keep it from covering his eyes), I vacuumed the interior of my car while it was parked in the hot garage, I even picked up around the house because I detest messes. But I used to be able to do these things and be able to walk with ease. It's getting harder and harder to live with this disease.

Rick does what he can to improve the situation by taking me on wonderful trips, and to shows and concerts, but I dislike having to share this illness with him. I don't want to share it with *anybody*.

Last night, we went to a luau in Fort Lauderdale. We had a great time. We wore the matching outfits we purchased in Hawaii. A few weeks ago, we went to New York for three nights, which turned into four nights when our flight was canceled. Of course, we simply managed to enjoy ourselves for one more night. We went to a Broadway show each night to soak in the marvelous musicals. I needed my wheelchair for most of the vacation. I loathed being in New York and having to sit instead of stand and walk. It was flattering to be asked if I was a model or actress. When I'm in the chair I feel so *not* like either of those. I just have to tell myself, It could be worse, right? I'm grateful to be going on vacations with or without a wheelchair! I'm making an effort to be upbeat, but it is grueling! I'm distraught.

Sandy, my neighbor down the street with MS, called me the other day. She is gloomy because she has to stop teaching because of the illness. She's sixty. I told her I'd been nineteen when MS started taking my life plans away. I didn't mean to be insensitive. I *know* how difficult this is for her. I totally understand. I just wish I didn't have so much in common with a woman twice my age, you know? I have to stay optimistic for myself and those who love me. Oh, I didn't mention how re-markable the Mark Anthony concert was. His voice is anything but ordinary. I love Rick for sharing my salsa dance infatuation with me!

Wednesday, August 2, 2000

My father came over last night with Rosalinda and my little sister, Amaris. It was a nice visit. I haven't seen them since Christmas. They hadn't been to my house in *years*. Thankfully, Rick's dad calls me often to ask how I feel. That makes me feel all warm inside! He asked me about my dad. I told him he's a busy man, so I don't talk to him often. You know what Dad Capozzi said? I will never forget when he told me, "He doesn't know what he's missing." Wow. He brought tears to my eyes. I needed that, I just didn't know how much.

Friday, August 4, 2000

I feel yucky today. My legs are weak. At least I'm not in the hospital! That's me, looking for good news.

Saturday, August 19, 2000

I had to write about all the vacations we have planned before the end of the year. In September we are going to Seattle/Vancouver for a week. In October we will drive to Key West to stay for three nights. Decem-ber finds us back in New York for the various Christmas festivities. I'm worn out just thinking about it! I am ex-cited but, at the same time, want to *walk* it all. I know it's a lot of walking, but that's what miracles are for. I'm hoping to feel better, but if not, at least I'll have a new little wheelchair.

Friday, August 25, 2000

I went to an MS support group last night. Being there makes me have to face the fact that I have an incurable disease. Reality bites. Honestly, I have to find a way that makes my life livable. Sure, this is a tough fight, but I'm not a quitter. Giving up would be way too easy. That just tells me it's the wrong thing to do. I will continue to make each moment count. I deal with this existence the best way I know how. I'm content with that—and it's really all that matters to me anyway. Live today as if it was your last.

I maintain a cheery behavior, making this life look so easy, but Lord, it is problematic. The more I share with individuals about how I actually feel and how truly difficult my life is, the further I push them away and the lonelier I get. I get the impression this must be hell on earth.

Rick continues to take me on these wonderful vacations, which keeps my mind off my illness, but I'm walking less and less and using the wheelchair more and more. I think any stress is harmful to the MS. I think the stress of packing, planning, getting off schedule from the usual, being somewhere else, all that is stress! I enjoy the trips, but I need to pace myself. It's not my preference; it's more a necessity—today, anyway. I believe the trips are stress-relief for him as well. I don't recall *ever* voicing vacations as a *must* to be with me. I truly prefer individuals to show kindness and sincerity towards me; that's really all. It's that Be Nice to Me and I Easily Return the Gesture rule that I believe in. See? Simple. Life is tough enough for all of us!

Saturday, August 26, 2000

I'm having a little trouble breathing today. It's not really stopping me from doing things like laundry. It *does* make doing what I do *trickier*. I'm sleeping at night, but I don't get the impression I am rested. I believe it is more fatigue than sleeplessness. One day at a time: That's how I have to live with this disease.

Sunday, September 3, 2000

I can't believe I fell again. Rick and I were at Bloomingdale's. I was in the wheelchair for the most part. I got up for a moment to walk around looking for a blouse. As I made my way to the fitting room, I noticed my legs getting number and number, as if I had just been given anesthesia. Then I just fell. Rick was right behind me with the wheelchair, though, and I was ambulating with a cane, so it wasn't as if I had no support.

My knee hurts more today than it did yesterday. Unfortunately, it's the same knee I tore a ligament in last November. I was finally comfortable without the knee brace. It had been feeling pretty good. Ah, the life of an MSer!

Monday, September 4, 2000

How do I feel today? I *felt* pretty good when I got up! It was the usual 6:30 a.m. I felt rested. I was ambulating fairly well (for me). I proceeded to organize my clothes I wanted to pack for our trip to Seattle. That wiped me out. My legs are so done. I get clumsier and weaker as I increase my activity. It sucks. I just want to cry. I can barely walk in shoes. I drag my legs more as I walk more. I purchased an ankle brace at Walgreen's. I saw it there last week and thought, Maybe it will help support my weak right ankle? I'm wearing it now. It's reasonably comfortable. It's soft, and it laces it, so it is less cumbersome. I figure that any help is good. I often attempt to be creative in my battle to disguise my disability. I'm sad. I'm lonely. People don't want to talk to me too much because of my speech impairment. I'm stubbornly fighting this *thing* that has dared for so long to invade my body. I continue focusing on the many trips, both in the past and those trips to come. I hope Rick can hang in there through this fight. I dislike what it does to him. I don't want to hurt him or my mother. Do they realize how important they are to me and my sanity? I don't know what I would do without them. They are the only ones who call me every day to ask how I'm feeling. They actually want an honest answer! I'm comforted merely by hearing their voices each day. Hopefully, they are aware of how I equally am there for them. Having MS doesn't exclude me from being empathetic. You don't have to have MS to experience life's challenges. I get the privilege, though, of battling the same everyday problems they are confronted with *along with* struggling to live with the disease! I will do this, not because I want to, but because I have to.

Friday, September 9, 2000

We are getting closer to our vacation! We leave next week. I have the sensation I am cut in half. I'm walking on those golf balls again.

Friday, September 29, 2000

We had a *wonderful* three nights in Seattle! The weather was not quite as wet as anticipated. I walked so much; I didn't have time to feel ill! From there, we traveled to Victoria for a night. The flowers were such a sight, *beautiful*. Then we went to Vancouver for three nights. I really liked Vancouver. I could live there! I could give a much more elaborate description of our vacation, but suffice to say the trips were an experience I will treasure, and I made the best of my time regardless of having to share it with MS.

I am so tired, though. The trip exhausted me. I feel crappy. My legs don't work too well. Walking is difficult. I'm having trouble staying positive, but I can't let it get me down. Gee, do you think maybe I need to chill? Of *course* I'm exhausted, I recently returned from a vacation! Shouldn't I feel rested? Maybe now is *when* I should rest.

Two days ago, Rick and I went to a seminar about MS at JFK Hospital. Dr. Millan was attending it also. It was nice to see him. I haven't in several years. I wonder if seeing him affected him the way it did me. He is, after all, the doctor who diagnosed my MS. I wonder if he is looking at me and how the disease is affecting me. I don't feel that different—until I view myself through his eyes. Do I look the same? Does he feel sorry for me? Does he admire me because I keep going, living with an affliction dreaded by so many? I don't know. I suppose he just gives me a glancing thought and moves on. Most people can't give me, or MS, too much thought, because it makes them uncomfortable. I get the impression they are grateful they don't have to deal with it or me. I guess I can't blame them. It's hard anyhow to confront a situation you can't change. What I can say? I focus on what I'm grateful for. For example, take my shih-tzu sleeping on the floor: He's been with me no matter what. Also my mother, my husband, the few friends who can bear to listen to my awkward speech (Seattle is *Sattle*). That's kinda funny. *I* know I'm still Alys, the same Alys I was before MS joined me.

Monday, October 2, 2000

My house is so dirty. I can't stand it! (See, I'm still me. I want to clean it myself, but MS limits me. The more energy I expend, the clumsier I get. I couldn't stand the dusty tables, rugs that needed vacuuming, the dusty T.V. screen, so I cleaned it all! It took a whole twenty minutes. When I was done, I could barely walk, but I sure was satisfied with a cleaner house!

Monday, October 23, 2000

We had so much fun at Key West this weekend! We partied both Friday and Saturday night until 1:00 to 2:00 a.m. I'm beat, but it was worth it! MS will pay me back later, but I have no regrets. I cleaned the bathrooms and floors before we left, which left my legs wiped out, but I walked Key West anyway. I was determined to, cane in one hand, husband in the other. I rarely used the wheelchair even though there were many times I could have. I just wanted to be normal. We stayed at our Ocean Key Resort overlooking Mallory Square. A Latin band was next door each night. Loved it!

Of course, now, I just need to recoup. I've been going to the gym for the past two weeks one or two times a week. It feels good to get back to some sort of a routine.

Tuesday, October 31, 2000

It's Halloween. It's raining. We enjoy celebrating, even though we don't have kids. The house is decorated with Halloween decor the way we like to do it! It's fun to see kids all decked out with their costumes. We have new neighbors since Dave moved out following Tara's passing.

Wednesday, November 1, 2000

I can't believe it's November! I'm feeling pretty good. I'm glad I've been going to the gym. I like working out a little and meeting new people as well as seeing familiar faces.

November 12, 2000

Yesterday, Samantha and I went to Boca Raton to attend a meeting sponsored by the MS Society, which featured physicians talking about the latest treatment for MS. David Lander, who played Squiggy on the sitcom *Laverne & Shirley*, was also a speaker. He spoke about his MS diagnosis and promoted his book about it. He was quite funny. After he spoke, we took pictures and had our book signed by him. We also spent more time speaking to him. I showed him how I use hair ties to secure my low-heeled, slip-on (so stylish— *ha*) red shoes from sliding off my feet. Really, I just wanted to show him how adapting to this life-changing diagnosis *can* be managed. He didn't say it, but I've been there, and I know this was not part of his plan!

After we finished there, we went to downtown West Palm Beach, where there were protesters and oth-

With David Lander—best known for playing Squiggy on the TV show
Laverne and Shirley, *when he spoke at an MS seminar*
about his book on the illness.

ers peacefully gathered in front where the voter hand-
count was occurring. I took some pictures because,
after all, this is history in the making! We went a couple of days ago when Jesse Jackson was there, along
with three thousand other people. I am confident that
this wonderful country will resolve this matter, and
that we will survive regardless of who eventually wins.
God Bless America.

November 18, 2000

Well, we still don't know who will be the forty-third President of the United States of America. Both sides keep going at it. To me, this is democracy at its best. Still, many are growing impatient and wonder who our next President will be.

Anyway, I'm feeling okay. I got a good workout in the gym. I've been meeting a lot of people there. I have more energy for whatever reason so I'm using it to exercise.

11:00 a.m.: I just fell down yet again. I was sitting here in the back room, reading David Lander's book, when I had to get up quickly to go to the bathroom. All of a sudden, I was dizzy and fell on my right wrist, then my left knee.

I *hate* this disease. Sometimes something as simple as standing up can be problematic. I take a deep breath and regroup to embrace encouraging thoughts.

January 3, 2001

We had a fabulous time in Orlando for New Year's Eve. We stayed at Portofino Bay in Universal Studios. We have stayed there before, so it was familiar and comfortable. It was certainly less stress for *me!* Staying there reminds us of our honeymoon in Italy. I actually got to wear long pants, a sweater, and even a coat! It's that cold in Orlando. Love it! I even wear gloves for my cold hands. I'm walking with a cane, but my body enjoys the cold weather—a nice break from the heat and humidity so common in Florida.

My speech has returned to usual, I'm breathing with ease, and I'm happy. I'm looking forward to starting the New Year with gusto!

I also can't wait until I finish writing this journal. I'm almost done with it, which is good, because my handwriting is sloppy. The journal has been my good companion, always there for me. That must mean it is time for a change, I guess. I don't know. I'm thinking I should just pray for direction. I calmly do: "God," I say, "why am I here? I mean, I thought being a registered nurse was a good plan. It's not like I'm raising a child, so what's the plan? What's *Your* plan?

13

ANSWER

February 2, 2001

I feel *different*, never this way before, *never*. I mean, if I was asked how I am feeling today, I would probably give the question some thought, then answer, "different."

Seriously, I have reason to answer this question any other way. I guess I'm happy. One point that comes to mind is how content I am right now. I don't have outstanding concerns that require my undivided attention, no active symptoms or life-changing events. I can't think of any other responsibilities I need to handle.

So I'm going to the store today, because I can! I want to get out of the house.

I make my way to Wal-Mart to look around. After I tour the store, I stop at a shelf with home pregnancy tests on it. I think, *Why not?* and shrug. I buy a package and take it home. I figure it won't hurt to check.

I take it home, complete the test, and *wow!* I am pleasantly surprised when I see a (+) result!

I can hardly wait to share my news with Rick. Immediately, I reach for the phone. . .then pause. I don't want to share this with him on the *phone*.

Plan B, Mami. I call my mom, who is at work. I cry happy tears. I quickly assure her it's about good news, I'm pregnant! She immediately hangs up and comes over, delighted—as evidenced by a warm hug. We go to lunch (because I'm eating for two now), and spend the rest of the afternoon together.

Later that night, when Rick (a.k.a. "Daddy," now) came home, I barely let him in the door before I told him I was pregnant. He seemed joyful as well. All right, he was truly happy, maybe slightly concerned about how the pregnancy would affect our lives now involving a child as well. That is when having faith is truly tested. My mom was somewhat concerned as well, but I believe in me, God, and I truly am going to do my best to be a good—no, great—mom. I will do this. I believe anxiety shows no faith.

To be completely sure, the next day I bought three more pregnancy tests made by other companies to convince myself it was actually happening. Silly, but I had to be certain before telling others. We waited until after my doctor's appointment three days later to spread the word. Rick wore a pin on his shirt containing a teddy bear and building blocks when he went to work.

My very first sonogram was done at six weeks. Rick was at work, so my mother went with me. I saw a figure on the screen as the device slid around my belly. There it was-an object I could see in my abdomen about the size of a pea! It was really there. It had been confirmed. Mom and I looked at each other as I teared up.

During my pregnancy, I was flooded with emotions. I felt happy, excited, nervous, and thrilled. I just want to be a good mother. All went well, even with a few bumps in the road. I had two exacerbations during it, but I refused to treat them with medication—I was not willing to expose my child to medication for ME, not the tiny life growing inside of me. Dr. Sheremata was out of town when I had my first MS attack and I chose thus not to treat with meds. When he got back, though, he said, "Good girl." My second MS attack was near the end of my pregnancy. I eventually got through the attacks with minimal complications. It was increasingly difficult, however, to balance myself with a growing belly. I was told by the doctor who was going to deliver this child, "Perhaps an electric chair will prevent more falls. If you keep falling, you run the risk of losing your child." So I have a new mission. I traded my current SUV for one that could accommodate a power chair. I refused to get a van. I find an SUV that I felt was not associated with *disability!* I don't care much for needing it— but this is about my baby, not me. I gathered the guts to get a power chair, too, which I use often when I drive myself to the store (to shop for baby items, of course). I stuck a sign on the back of the chair that read *Baby on Board!*

I am enjoying this time of my life. Women are often diagnosed with MS following pregnancy; having it happen in the reverse order is not so common. Dr. Sheremata says I have already had my post-pregnancy exacerbation, so he doesn't expect me to have one after the birth of my child.

Thankfully he was right: I had a decent pregnancy, though I was hospitalized when I couldn't keep food down at about four months into the pregnancy. The morning sickness was 24/7 sickness for me!

I was frequently referred to as looking like a beach ball with legs. I remained thin but gained weight in the belly. I had a picture of myself taken each month, holding up as many fingers as corresponded to it. That way my child would be able later to see how Mommy's appearance had changed to accommodate a growing fetus. Also, I could say to you one day, "See? You were there with me." I was making memories for the person we had created.

My cravings during pregnancy included Oreo cookies, McDonald's strawberry shakes with their French fries, frequent meals at restaurants like Red Lobster, Pollo Tropical, and subs at Jon Smith Subs.

May 2, 2001

I had a sonogram. As I looked at the screen, I commented, "Your profile looks just like your father's!" As the months passed I had more sonograms to check the progress of the fetus. Each time I saw you growing, I was told you were healthy. "Do you want to know the sex?" I shook my head to tell them I didn't, with a grin in my face. I wanted a healthy baby, period, and didn't care either way about the gender. As I patiently awaited your arrival, I spent my time reading about pregnancy, doing exercises, mostly yoga, playing music with headphones on my belly (I felt you move mostly when still or resting, or when I played my Santana CD), I often read bedtime stories to you or just talked to you as if you understood what I was saying.

I spent time looking up names for a boy or a girl. I liked seeing what the web showed for popular names and I altering them a little so they were unique. If you were a boy, I'd always liked Christian, but that was too common for me and your cousin is Chris, so that was out. If you were a girl, I liked Gabriella but I still wanted to change it just a little. Rick didn't particularly care what the name would be, so I'd do the research!

We finally chose a name for each sex: Tristian Julius (T.J.) and Abrielle Cha'ree. Tris or Bri for short. That was enjoyable! Really, once the names had been picked, I wondered, now what? I suppose I will prepare for the time I will be spending in the hospital.

I was determined to be prepared for anything.

14

FOCUS

September 18, 2001

"Where is anesthesia," I anxiously asked the nurse as I was lying in my assigned hospital bed. I was tired. Earlier that evening I had repeatedly awakened, getting out of bed to use the bathroom. I must have eaten something that hadn't agreed with me. It felt like cramps. As I continued to get out of bed, my husband had asked, "What's the matter? Are you okay?"

I'd told him in a groggy voice, "Every time I start falling asleep, I feel as though I have to go to the bathroom. I just want to *sleep*. I'm having a baby any *day* now. I need to be *rested*."

He had laid his hand on my belly. A moment later, I'd moaned, "Oooh! See? I just can't get any rest!"

He'd removed the hand. I few minutes later, I had felt it and moaned again. He'd touched my belly again and said, with a concerned look on his face, "I think you're having contractions."

"No!" I had exclaimed impatiently. "I'm not having *pain*. I just need to use the *bathroom*."

Moments later, I had moaned once more, looked into his eyes, and gasped, "I think I'm having contractions! That felt a little more serious!"

He'd called the hospital and told them what was happening.

They'd told him, "She needs to come in."

"Come on," he had said.

I hadn't wanted to go *anywhere*, just sleep, and dreaded the thought of going to the hospital just to be told I was having false labor pains. However, I'd known I needed to go, so we had.

"Wake my mother and tell her we're going," I'd said to him. So he'd gone to her room and told her we were leaving while I slipped out of my pajamas and slid into my denim maternity dress with white Keds on my feet. My long, dark brown hair had been a mess, as if I had just gotten out of bed, which of course I had.

We had made our way to our car: 3:00 a.m., pitch-black outside, perfect for *sleeping!* I had grumbled.

Driving as if we are going to have a baby, Rick had quickly gotten us to Palms West Hospital, twelve miles away from Mom's house. (We'd moved into her house because our house had sold sooner than we expected.

Okay, maybe we should have waited until the baby was born to move—after all, we had just finished remodeling our house. But having a baby is reason enough to move, right? More about that later: I'm going to have a *baby!*)

As I was saying, once we got to the hospital, Rick had grabbed a wheelchair, and we were off! He'd rushed me through the E.R., following directions from the receptionist, my contractions getting more frequent. When we reached my assigned room, I'd stopped one last time at the bathroom just inside the doorway.

Then my water broke! *What timing*, I had said to myself.

"Any later, you'd had the baby in the car!" the nurse told us.

I'd gotten got into a hospital gown and carefully got into bed; I had more contractions, pain.

"Where's *anesthesia?*" I asked the nurse again as the contractions get more painful.

"We have no order for that," she said.

"What?" That couldn't be. The planning, preparation, organization, meeting with anesthesia, the hospital tour, Lamaze classes—I'd even packed a small bag with music I enjoy listening to. "Ohhhh!" The pain was getting worse.

She gave me a Tordal tablet for pain and checked my progress as I yelled, *"Ohhhh!"* again and asked, "Where's *anesthesia?* "

"Push!" she ordered.

"*What?*"

"*Push!* I see the head! Your baby is coming!"

This couldn't be happening so quickly. My doctor was going out of town. My due date was ten days away. "Did you call the on-call doc?" I asked nervously.

"She hasn't returned the call, so we called your doctor, Dr. Pliskow."

Just then the phone rang. It was him. "Okay," I heard her say, and she hung up.

Meanwhile, I was pushing. I wanted the baby out! She said. "Okay. Stop pushing."

"What? Why?"

"He's on his way."

I looked at her in frustration, thinking, Are you *kidding* me?

Thank God I'd been given a mild medication for pain, since anesthesia couldn't give me anything. I was so tired, sleeping between contractions, and they were so *painful,* nothing like what I read about regarding labor pain. Nothing! They actually felt like cramps at first. But that had escalated into pain I had never experienced.

Focus, I told myself. Breathe—in through the nose, out through the mouth. I told myself, Women have been doing this for*ever*. I can do this. I wish the doctor would hurry! It seems like forever.

Finally, there he was—and here it came! We didn't

know if it was a boy or girl. The umbilical cord was in the way during ultrasound, so they couldn't tell me for sure. I didn't care. I just wanted a healthy child. . .and to stop referring to it as *it!*

"*It's a boy!*" the doctor said.

After cleaning and wrapping you up in a blanket, they lay you in my arms. You haven't stopped crying. "Shhh," I gently whisper as I cradle you close to me. You appear to calm down— the stranger who is going to change my life, I think.

Now the real challenge begins. I know *nothing* about raising a boy. He's beautiful. He looks nothing like what we expected. Red hair! What a perfectly round head. He's perfect. He's mine (I mean ours—ha). So *this* is God's plan.

I'm ready to go home. I'm done, sleepy; I'm ready for the next phase of my life. I'm glad I didn't get anesthesia, for his sake and mine.

I knew I would be alright, but wow, I am *wide awake* for this experience, and he easily accepts being nursed by Mommy. As I am awakened nightly for your feeding, I am oblivious of how much sleep deprivation I have endured. We are visited by family and friends for the two days and two nights at the hospital.

As we prepare to get in the SUV, complete now with a baby car seat, I think , They're going to let us just *leave?* I know this is how it's done. But *I* have never done it before!

We're going back to Mom's house, a two-bedroom, two-bath single family. She lives alone now. Our new house was supposed to be ready by now. That was *that* plan.

She's at work when we get there, so we get a little quality time alone with our new arrival. We are staying in a room that smaller than our previous two-car garage. Formerly, it was my bedroom. Now, it's ours—one side for baby, and our queen-size bed on the other. I can't believe we managed to fit in the plastic drawers for our clothes and dedicated an entire wall to the baby, complete with changing table, plastic drawers for infant essentials, and of course, a wall decorated in baby décor. The bassinet is decked out for its prince. It has a fabric canopy that can be closed when baby is resting. It is large, so he can grow and sleep close to me. I want to be a family, just the three of us, but the house is crowded with many items from the baby shower, not to mention our invasion of my mom's home. Bless her for allowing us to stay.

Of course, she is tolerating her new grandson, but we don't want to overstay our welcome, so we spend ten more days and, afterwards, end up moving to a large one-bedroom apartment closer to our new home. They have agreed with the developer of our new place to allow us to rent there on a monthly basis. Many of our soon-to-be neighbors are staying there as well. It is next to

WRMC. I can see the hospital every day from our window and be reminded of my time working there.

As I sit in the rocking recliner, looking at you, Tristian, lying in my arms, I smile. All is good.

We manage to transfer many items that were in storage, like our living room furniture, dining room furniture, even our king size bed! *Aahh.* Soon the apartment begins to feel like home. There is even a well-equipped gym we visit on occasion. Zubi seems calm, almost uninterested in the new addition to our family. I reassure him how much he means to me.

October 19, 2001

I have a cast on my left leg covering my left foot and ankle. I broke my left big toe when I got up from our table at lunch yesterday. I stood up after lunch and heard a pop. I thought it was my left ankle. When I woke up this morning, I couldn't stand on that foot. My toe is ugly, bruised and swollen.

What next? I am exhausted from the nightly breast feedings. We went to the ER at WRMC, where they X-rayed it and casted it for me. So here I am caring for an infant while recovering from childbirth, and breast feeding every two to three hours, wearing a cast more or less the size of Tristian. I continue to bathe, change diapers for, feed, read and talk to, and love my son. I can do this. The MS is not bothering me currently. I don't want others to take care of my child. I'm okay. Rick is working,

With a cast on my leg the size of one-month-old Tristian

often. He bottle-feeds Tristian occasionally before leaving for work so I can get more than two hours of sleep at a time. Tris does well with feedings, I think; he just wants to eat! I'm sure Rick enjoys spending time with him.

Zubi is quiet. He randomly urinates on the carpet. This behavior is uncommon for him. I love him so much but it is tough to care for him and Tristian as well. My mother offers to keep him at her home. He will be loved, I'm sure. He does well with her, so I agree to let him stay with her.

One night I get a call from her. She tells me that he was ill, and that she took him to the animal hospital, where he was diagnosed with an incurable kidney ailment. He needs to be put down.

This news is hard to comprehend. I don't want to agree to it, but I know he has been suffering. Zubi was my first child, always happy to see me, wagging his tail and jumping in my lap, so I could pet him and run my fingers through his fur. I didn't see my future without him. *I miss him.*

February 14, 2002

I feel well today. I just gave Tristian a bath. He rolled over twice today! I give him tummy time each day, and today he rolled over! He has been babbling and laughing often. I tell him, smiling, "You are funny, aren't you?" I refer him as Mr. Talkalot. He is babbling like crazy. I love it!

April 8, 2002 Monday

Our son is six months old when we move into our new home. It is a spacious four-bedroom, three-bath with a den. From the double-door entry, the dining room is to the left, the den is to the right. The master is at one end, the other rooms at the other. The ceilings are high, and there's a sunken living room.

Up to now, Tris has been sleeping in the bassinet. The furniture for his room has now been delivered. He gets to sleep in his crib, in his room, at the other end of our house.

I am uncomfortable having my baby so far away. We get a camera, so I can see him from our bedroom if he is crying or whatever. It's the greatest thing! Rick turns on the T.V. before leaving for work, and I can see my son sleeping peacefully. Tristian is a good baby— thank goodness, because I'm not feeling so hot. I'm waking up in the morning but feeling fatigued, not rested. I eventually get the courage to restart the Alferon, hoping I will feel better.

Days turn into months. I am so fatigued, but I suppose it's because I had a baby. The pain in my fingers, hands, and most of my joints is getting to be unbearable. I am seen by a local rheumatologist, but he is concerned with my swollen ankles, even though I continue to point out my fingers and their terrible pain. I tell him, "I know my ankles are swollen, but my concern is the constant pain in my *hands*." He gives me a prescription for a pain med that has just been approved by the FDA. I insist I need a diagnosis and treatment for whatever is *causing* this pain. (The med he prescribed for my pain was later recalled due to severe side effects shortly after I he gave me the prescription. Thankfully, I never took it.)

September 21, 2002

My baby is talking so much. He repeats everything in both English *and* Spanish. His favorites are: *rico* (yummy), *agua* (water), *flat, Bob* (the builder), *open, corn* (popcorn), *apple sauce, hugs and kisses*, and *stuffed animals*.

He loves everything. He is very affectionate.

(As he got older, when he spoke Spanish words, he had that Spanish accent, not like an American trying to speak Spanish! He now speaks more English than Spanish, even though he understands me when I speak Spanish to him. As he has matured, his fair skin and auburn hair are *so* not like his parents' tannable skin and dark brown hair!

Friday, October 3, 2003

My son said, "I love you!" When I put him down for his nap, I looked him in the eyes, grinning, and said to him, "I love you," and he repeated what I said!

This shows me how important it is to be mindful of what I say in the presence of children, as they duplicate our words and behavior.

October 22, 2003

I call Dr. Sheremata's office and describe the pain to his nurse. I know it's not MS pain. I have never had it before. I am in tears and begging for someone to acknowledge it and my red knuckles. I don't need a pain killer; I need a diagnosis to treat an illness *and* a pain killer!

I am begging Dr. Sheremata to send me to a rheumatologist. The nurse tells me Maldonado's husband is a rheumatologist; maybe she can get me an appointment to see him. I assume Maldonado is a secretary or nurse that works for Dr. Sheremata. All I know is she works there in Dr. Sheremata's office, and I trust the nurse, and U of M, so I'll take any help right now!

I get an appointment with Dr. M. Maldonado weeks later. Struggling with the pain and MS, I finally see him. He is about my age, with dark brown hair. He is kind and easy to talk to. Rheumatoid arthritis—that's the diagnosis for this joint pain. He immediately focuses his attention on the hands resting on my lap and tells me, "You have arthritis."

"What?" I look at him inquisitively.

"The arthritis young people can get." He also assesses my swollen ankles and tells me they are being caused by the same condition. He explains it to me and gives me a prescription for Prednisone. He tells me it should help the pain until I can be placed on a medication to treat rheumatoid arthritis long term.

I start on a very low dose but feel no relief. I call his office and leave a message with his assistant that I'm going to increase the dose. "Call me back if it is a problem," I say. I have been on Prednisone before, so I am familiar with the side effects.

November 7, 2003

My joints feel as though they have been replaced with cement. I'm ready to increase the Prednisone to 15 mg. I can't believe I started at 5 mg without relief.

I eventually increase the dose to a level comfortable

for me. Ah, *relief*. But it is short lived, and I am aware that I can't be on Prednisone long term, so Dr. Maldonado and I discuss long-term treatment. The choices are limited for me, since I also have MS and I am treating that with medication as well. We decide on methotrexate. It is chemo—just another reason to fight fatigue. Joy.

Why is this happening to me?

Eventually, Sheremata's nurse tells me that I need to find another physician to replace Dr. Sheremata, since he recently had open heart surgery and is now semi-retired. I ask her if she has any recommendations at the university. She mentions a few names, one of them, Dr. Janice Maldonado. This is when I realize Maldonado is a doctor! Then I realize *both* Maldonados are doctors! When Janice Maldonado sees me, I am instantly pleased by the personality coming from the young brunette about my age, and I am pleased she as easy to talk to as her husband was. She remains my neurologist to this day. I like her. Her husband has left U of M, though, so he no longer practices there.

15

ONE, TWO, THREE, FOUR PRE-K

One

September 14, 2002

Well, life goes on regardless of how I feel, so I continue to make the best of each situation. Tristian is turning a year old soon. My, how time flies. I am so grateful he is a good child. I am experiencing severe pain, mostly in my hands. It hurts to touch or move my fingers. The pain makes it quite challenging to care for my child, but I face this situation with all the strength I can. He sleeps through the night; he doesn't fuss about situations many children his age do. He seems happy, content, and keeps surprising me with how he handles his life. I continue to do my best to handle mine. Luckily, he just keeps me smiling as I am confronted with difficult symptoms like pain in my joints, along with weakness and fatigue.

This pain has subsided somewhat. I couldn't take Alferon *and* methotrexate—the side-effects of fatigue and weakness were too great—so I am solely on chemo for now. I do my best to keep my problems from Tris. He doesn't need to see Mommy struggle to be normal. I won't cry in front of him. I won't be anything but be a good example for him. I want what's best for him. He is too young to have to deal with or understand what I'm going through anyway.

I'm still making memories, good memories, like when he laughs at me as I speak Spanish words. I call him *niño lindo* ("beautiful boy" in Spanish) with a smile on my face as I tickle him, with my long hair brushing his cheeks, while he lies in his stroller. If I accomplish anything during these years of his life, I hope he learns how much we control our own life, memories, and actions based on our own choices. He is too young to know that now, but as he gets older, I can honestly say, "See? It's not impossible—difficult but not impossible!" I want him to learn from my behavior how I dealt with these times of adversity so he can recall optimistic behavior when confronted with whatever challenges he may face. I believe these years are a vital time for children as they absorb information like a sponge.

We celebrated his birthday today with a party at our

home. It was nice to be with family and friends. I hide my troubles well. If I am asked how I feel, I respond "fine" or "good." I have a smile on my face and continue to enjoy this festive event. This day is not about me, it's about him. He exhibits expected growing milestones and more at times. He enjoys playing with age-appropriate toys as well as more difficult ones. I enjoy speaking to him as though he understands; he seems to be interested in whatever I have to say.

Two

Bob the Builder—that's the theme for Tristian's second birthday party. He enjoys himself; he and his friends all have yellow Bob construction hats for the party. They do their best to knock down the Bob piñata, which is filled with candy. Tristian gets pleasure out of playing with just about anything. We got him a Bob the Builder stuffed character that is bigger than he is. He appears to enjoy building towers with whatever he lays his hands on. I am bracing myself for the so-called Terrible Twos. He continues to be a joy, to be disciplined and a pleasure to spend time with, as I continue to fight fatigue. When we are home, he spends much of his time in a child-fenced area, which occupies most of our family room. He has an abundance of toys in there that keep him stimulated both mentally and physically. I am aware of his activity throughout the day. We have baby-proofed cabinets, electrical outlets, and he actually obeys when I say, "No," as he attempts to open locked cabinets or tries to touch an outlet. Locks on doors are high, so he can't go out without an adult. We fenced in our back-yard to prevent him from running out in the street. I am firm with my orders but praise him when he displays positive behavior. I am constantly aware of his actions as I make raising him as close to normal as possible while his mommy confronts the MS, rheumatoid arthritis, and thyroid disease, all of which feature fatigue as their major symptom, on a daily basis. Let's not forget I am on chemotherapy as well!

Three

Yippy! Potty training a success! I even bought him a book to read with pictures to teach him all about it! That was easy. He learns quickly, thank God. That was as easy as when he gave up the *te-te* ("pacifier" in Span-ish). They call it a pacifier for a reason, right? It appears to pacify him when he appears distressed. I hear about parents taking it from there child before they are ready to give it up. So, I just let him feel as though it was his decision! That seems like so long ago. We talked about it; I said, "Aren't you ready to get rid of that?" pointing to the pacifier dangling from his shirt where it was pinned. He agreed and threw it away.

So now the potty training is done—now what? I

show him how we can find things on the computer, like Disney World web sites so we can make Mickey Mouse ears out of paper and play other games on the computer for his age. We entertain his large selection of educational toys as well as silly toys (Sponge Bob, Spiderman, and many toy trucks). He continues to make raising a child rewarding as I watch him grow up.

September 2, 2004

Rick has put up the hurricane shutters. This is one of four hurricanes we have had this year in Florida. My mother, as well as my sister and my niece and nephew, Hanna and Joshua, stay at our home, which is new and strong, so we feel comfortable in it. Most importantly, we are with family.

We fare well during the hurricanes. I am hot and really anxious for the air conditioning to be on. The cold showers are uncomfortable, the food is bearable, and I love having a microwave! We share a generator with our next-door neighbor, which we use sporadically. I am handling the heat better than I thought I would. Not for long, though. I carry ice packs constantly to cool me off. The refrigerator is on generator, plus we have an Igloo. The stress on my mind and body are hard to handle, but I know it could be worse. I know I have a roof over my head, food to survive, and water. Many others are without some or all of these essentials for survival. Get it? I'm thinking positive thoughts!

September 16, 2004

Why not go on vacation? Tris will be turning three, so we decide to celebrate at Universal Studios. While staying at the hotel, we have dinner at one of their restaurants. He is visited by characters like Sponge Bob, Woody Woodpecker, and his favorite, Scooby Doo. I love to see the reaction on his face as he gets balloons from them, especially Scooby Doo, his favorite! I'm tolerating the trip. I'm just really tired but, come on, he only turns three once!

September 18, 2004

We had a *super* time at Universal, today is Tris's actual birthday, and we are driving back home. "Look over there!" Rick points out the caravan of FPL trucks heading north to assist with restoring power elsewhere. Our state is between hurricanes. We must be nuts! How did we manage to take a vacation under these circumstances? We learn how important each day is.

When we get home, of course, we give Tristian the birthday presents we bought for him. Wrapped in Scooby Doo wrapping paper, we gave him a Matchbox race track and a toy computer. He spends endless hours with the race track until it breaks, then even more time trying to fix it! (The computer will endure many for years, until it is replaced with a laptop for kids.)

Halloween, October 31, 2004

Tristian dressed up as Sponge Bob, and his father walked with him in Sponge Bob attire. I even dressed up for Halloween, wearing my cheer-leading uniform complete with pompoms. It was a lot of work to dress up and hand out candy. I could have stayed in the house, but I want to participate in this holiday because I can! My uniform is orange and black, so it fits right in for Halloween. Do I still fit into it? Well, actually, yes—but it is short, so I wear my lancerette uniform instead, since it is more recent and in the same colors, and my saddle shoes actually fit! I'm thin because I have little appetite. The chemo assists very effectively with the appetite situation.

December 4, 2004

Scott's mom and sister visited my home; my mother was there as well. Rick is at work. It was a nice visit; Scott would be happy that we stay in touch. I have missed them. I'm sure we are all wishing Scott was with us as well. He is here in spirit. I have yet to admit that I lost the beautiful bracelet Scott gave me. Each time I see his mother, I look at the same bracelet she wears with a "J" on it for her first name. It breaks my heart to see the bracelet. I would replace it if I knew where he bought it!

December 24, 2004

Christmas Eve was familiar as we gathered with our family to celebrate. I am grateful it is at our house, where it is easy for me to get around, and I enjoy making the *lechon* and *flan,* and everyone else brings a dish to add to our buffet. "I like your boots," I am told at the party. As part of my outfit, I chose to wear boots because they support my ankles.

See? I can maintain some sort of style while I'm doing my best to join in the holiday spirit! I could always decide against having this at our home. I could say I don't feel well (I don't), but I chose to do otherwise, because this was important. Too much time had passed since I saw many family members for various reasons. Tonight, most found a way to come and get together! (We ended up celebrating Noche Buena annually with plenty of food, family, and friends as well.)

April 24, 2005

The article I wrote for the *Palm Beach Post* about how your children treat you was published in the newspaper today! It was chosen as a runner-up, and I was given a gift dinner at a restaurant of my choice. It is easy to write about Tris's behavior towards me during my challenging times. I just have to brag about it! I recently promised him I will never spank, hit, slap, or harm him in any way. Ever! I express my love for him often and teach him, "How can I honestly tell you I love you while I hit you? That's not love." I was never spanked by my parents. I will, *and do,* find effective ways to discipline my child without crushing his self-esteem or giving him

THE PALM BEACH POST • SUNDAY, APRIL 24, 2005 MSL W C NC

SUNDAYS

FAMILY, FASHION, 45+ AND FUN!

A little charm for everyone!

COUNTDOWN TO MOTHER'S DAY

Because bragging about your kids is a birthright

TODAY'S RUNNER-UP

Alys Capozzi,
Royal Palm Beach

"I didn't think I wanted to be a mom. I wasn't trying to become pregnant. I have Multiple Sclerosis and take a lot of meds for it. Being pregnant and raising a child would be too stressful and challenging.

"I stopped taking the meds while I was pregnant. I didn't want my child to be affected by my meds. I just wanted a healthy child. After the pregnancy, I was diagnosed with severe rheumatoid arthritis. I used to need a cane occasionally and a wheelchair rarely;

now I am in the wheelchair more than not.

"My son is 3½ years old now. I didn't know you could love another person so deeply. He makes me laugh, he makes me want to make the most of every day, for him. He loves me unconditionally even if I can't do a lot of things other moms do.

"Instead, he helps me. He gets his juice out of the refrigerator. He opens and closes the window blinds. He helps me make his bed, answers the phone, helps me do the laundry, he even helps me get my legs in the wheelchair when I have trouble. He is also a gentleman, opening doors for me, picking flowers for me. And then there are all those hugs and a kisses.

"Yes, life is difficult and yes, it is

Alys Capozzi says son Tristan, 3, helps with chores made difficult by her multiple sclerosis.

challenging, but Tristan is worth every struggle I had to face as a result of my pregnancy.

"Would I do it again? You bet!"

The article I published in the Palm Beach Post, Sunday, April 24, 2005

reason to doubt his behavior. I will do my best to raise a confident, decent child. I say "I" because I can only be responsible for my own treatment of him. I want him to trust me. He needs to earn that trust from me. His father continues working, while I do my best at being a mom.

Four—Pre-K

It is quite difficult finding a pre-school for my child— not so much *finding* one as getting him *to and from* it! Sometimes I am faced with so many challenges, it can be most frustrating. I battle my condition on a daily basis. This is so difficult, because I feel this battle is all *mine.* So, Tristian's pre-school is here at home. Who cares more about his education, anyway? Rick continues to work as much as possible while I keep Tristian's schooling as close to typical as possible.

I have him on a schedule for the most part. First, work with anything he can learn from—for example, numbers, the alphabet, colors, whatever I can teach him; then play, with whatever he wants. I am grateful for this opportunity, which I would not have had if I was working. Oh, yeah, I *am* working; I'm just not getting paid—with money, anyway. The time I am spending with my child is priceless.

He appears to be very bright and wanting to learn about whatever. He enjoys watching the program *How*

It's Made on T.V. He started showing interest in the show when Rick and I went to the Canadian Rockies to celebrate our tenth wedding anniversary in 2003. That would explain why our child was less than impressed with the toys, including a brown bear puppet (we thought he would love it). Tris was not even two then. He *liked* the gifts, but my mother would tell us about how he was mesmerized by programs on the Discovery Channel, Science Channel, even PBS (you know, *Sesame Street*) as he carefully watched them. He soaks up the info, then relays it to anyone willing to listen. Who said T.V. was bad for children? Come on, doesn't everyone want to know how to make a clock or a cowboy hat, or a hockey pucks It doesn't matter what it is, he wants to learn about it. I encourage him always. He surprises me always.

Just outside the gates to our neighborhood stands a Baptist church school. We have been neglecting our visits to church, mostly because I'm not feeling well. I wanted to have him experience going to church on a regular basis. I thought he could attend this school while learning about the religion I was raised in, along with learning valuable traits such as respect, kindness, and obedience—the very ones I diligently encourage in him as I teach him by example to the best of my ability. Unfortunately, there is no pre-school. I was told by the pastor, "He can start in kindergarten and repeat it if he doesn't pass at this school, because it's private. That would be the year public schools would allow him to start kindergarten anyway."

Rick and I give this extensive thought. I am aware that it will cost money that we do not have, but under such circumstances, he comes first. We discuss this with the pastor, along with our concerns about Tris being the youngest child in his grade. I tell Rick how ready he is to be in school. We talk to Tristian about it, and he seems excited to go to school. He is all smiles!

Well, it can't hurt so here goes!

2006–2007—Kindergarten

September 18, 2006

Today is Tristian's first day of school. He turns five today, so he is able to start kindergarten at the private school. The school year started a few weeks ago, but he catches up to the class schedule without difficulty.

The students wear a uniform—dark blue pants with a collared white shirt topped off with a dark blue tie. He wears dress shoes as well. Girls wear dark blue dresses. My son looks so cute! I know it's not the usual kindergarten attire, but he has no problem dressing this way. To him, it's like dressing for church! He is eager to go. It is a small school so he is given plenty of attention and taught the necessary rules for children at this age. I am comfortable trusting the staff, whom we have met while attending the church. Tristian enjoys attending school. I am so grateful for the woman who gives him a ride to and from school every day.

I continue to endure the MS challenges I am faced with. I fatigue, I am generally weak all over, and I occasionally have pain in my left eye, which might as well be a stake going into it. At least the pain in my fingers is tolerable now. I have created a schedule to make this transition of going to school as easy as possible for Tristian and me. Rick works as much as possible; I do too, making sure Tris is ready each day for school. Buttoning his shirt day is so challenging when you have my hands! I got a tool to assist me with this simple task. I'm finding a way to make it work. I believe we are able as human beings to adapt to situations. I'll find a way to make this simple task simple for *me!* I want him to learn how to treat others and respect adults. He learns this as well as getting a decent education.

I exercise each morning before getting out of bed, then again before lunch with equipment we have in the den. I enjoy cooking, so, oftentimes, I'll cook dinner and put it in the refrigerator to be warmed up for later. I am too warm following my shower, so I cook before I shower, then have a Popsicle after I blow dry this headful of hair. I know I could drink water, but Popsicles are tastier! I am aware of how important it is to drink water, but that also means I'd better be close to a bathroom! Again, this is working for *me*. I dislike being dependent on anyone for anything, so I do whatever I can. I hold dear my beliefs and faith that what is happening to me is *up* to me. I mean, I must make decisions about how I will deal with my life and show my son how that is all about choices. As far as he is concerned, everyone's mom occasionally uses a wheelchair.

"No Halloween costumes?" I ask a staff member?

"We don't want to scare the little ones, so we dress up for other occasions."

Candy is exchanged for Easter, and they have a contest for Valentine's Day in which each boy collects the hearts that the girls have pinned to their uniform, and one with the most hearts wins. They attend chapel each week, where they also have a contest for the best joke. Tristian's joke won when he told it:

"What did the left eye say to the right eye?"

Answer: "There's something between us that smells!"

They also dress up for football team day or themes like Cowboys and Indians. They have innocent fun. I'll take it! He is happy, so I'm happy.

16

GRADE SCHOOL
First and Second Grade

Tristian is looking forward to going back to school. He graduated kindergarten after I was told by his kindergarten teacher how I could make passing easier for him by giving him responsibilities at home. She told me how responsibility leads to independence. I thought about how simple this would be for my son, seeing as I allow him to do many things not expected of children his age anyway. He makes his bed with my assistance; we get breakfast and clear the table together. He even helps open close the window blinds!

He does well this year, familiar with expectations for advancement to the next year.

The school is closing by the end of second grade, though. Finances are tough for just about everyone, as many students are going to public schools instead of private ones. I remember a parent telling me how each of her children had started at this school, then transferred to public schools. She went on to say, "It's is a good start for children before they're faced with having to make tough choices."

I nodded in agreement, because I knew what she meant. He will have to deal with others who may not have been given the same lessons in how to treat people or respect another. I am so grateful he has been given these valuable lessons, since I know he will learn on his own how to handle situations like bullying or being confronted with students of different backgrounds. So other schools may not dress up for award ceremonies; he may not get trophies each year for successfully completing honor roll assignments or be recognized for being a good student. What is most important to me is that he knows that you are in control of how you are treated by others.

July 31, 2005

We decide to take Tristian to the Dreher Park Zoo because they are having a Winter in July event with snow for kids to play in! Rick and I are excited about Tris witnessing this rare event in Florida.

When we get there, a mound of snow has been trucked in. What does Tris say? He points out the truck spewing ice and informs us, "That's not really snow you know. That's just a truck with ice." We tell him to have fun anyway as Rick and I look at each other with raised eyebrows. Tris has fun making snow balls—or "ice balls," as he reminds us.

September 20, 2005

We took Tristian to Walt Disney World for his birthday. We go there often because that's where Rick proposed to me, so we buy annual passes. We return each year to celebrate our engagement anniversary anyway. This trip was for Tristian, though. We also invited my mother because she constantly shows us her affection by being there for all of us. She *deserves* a vacation.

2009–2010—Third Grade

I'm holding my breath as the transition from private to public school begins with Tristian's third grade. I spoke with our neighbor, Linda, who works at the elementary school he will be attending. She is a teacher there. Her two children are older than Tris and longtime friends of his as well. Her daughter is still attending there; her son is now in middle school.

The school is located beyond the other gate of our neighborhood (we have two, one for residents and guests—that's where Southwide Academy is; the other gate is solely for residents, and this is the one we use for public school). Linda, who lives behind us, recommended another neighbor, who also works there, to perhaps give my son a ride to school. She lives on our street.

When I meet Joanna, I am comfortable with her. She is sweet and easily agrees to give Tristian a ride to school. She has a son Tristian's age who rides his bike to school. Tristian would be riding *his* bike to school, but when he was learning, he fell hard when Dad let go of the bike, and he landed on the hard driveway next door. He insisted he would never get on a bike again! He was six at the time.

I would teach him bike-riding myself if I could run alongside him, but that would require actually running and balancing myself, which I'm having difficulty with. I tell him, "Hey, why don't we get you a kick scooter, and maybe you can learn to balance on that first?"

His best friend, Mathew, agrees that it would help and shows Tris how riding a scooter requires balance similar to bike riding. I'm thinking, Who else could possibly be dealing with such a basic duty as teaching a child how to ride a bike? Whatever, I'm determined to teach him!

Speaking to him calmly, I suggest we practice getting on the bike; I'm in the wheelchair, holding his bike seat steady while we are in the garage. He successfully accomplishes this. My sister comes over and helps him to learn by running next to him.

Until he rides his bike, he gets a ride from Joanna. When he doesn't get the ride, he walks with me at his side (in the wheelchair) to the gate, from which he continues to walk while I supervise until I see him cross the street to his school. I make my way back home until school is dismissed.

Once I am home, I'm often fatigued, but that's when I do my morning exercise. I can't wait to get out of the chair and stand, move, anything but sit! I work out before getting out of bed, then again after Tris is at school. My main symptom since childbirth has been fatigue. Still, I have learned to prioritize. My child comes first; then I can deal with cooking, cleaning, and issues related to MS. Oh yeah, I get to deal with MS issues every day! I used to put on makeup, lightly, leave the house for a while, socialize! Now I have learned what is really important. I no longer concern myself with how others see me. The way I see it, they must have issues that require their attention, and I'm pretty sure they have nothing to do with me!

We did not attend orientation prior to beginning this school. Actually, we didn't even know anything about it. We were told at the front desk while we filled out the paperwork, however, that his teacher would be calling us to tell us his room number and when we could go to meet his teachers and become familiar with his schedule and the expectations for passing the class.

Rick has to work, but Tris and I are going! It's important for both of us. Tris can become familiar with the school, and I can meet his teachers as well. Our situation is unique, as I quickly discover. When I say "unique," I'm talking about how we make our way to the school—Tris walking while I use the power chair. That's not all I'm talking about. Besides being the only parent in a power chair, parents are expected to fill out paper work for his first class. Not *writing*! My hands won't behave! His teacher, Ms. Wagner, is most understanding when I tell her how difficult writing is for me. She smiles at me with a relieving look. Ah, a kind person. She proceeds to write what I should be writing upon answering the questions.

This year has been quite a challenge for all of us. So this is what public school is like. I'm sure Tristian is thinking the same. He is given the opportunity to meet students from various backgrounds. He learns how differently teachers handle their classes. He has two different science teachers for third grade. I am happy with his first math/science teacher, Ms. Boss, because I am pleased with the organized way she manages to teach both third- and fourth-grade classes. The school is crowded, so, to keep the number of students at the required number per class, she is assigned to handle both grades in one room, yet she manages to keep a structured schedule for the children. She has students grade their homework for math, so they can see what they got wrong and correct the answers to prepare them for tests.

This procedure makes so much sense to me. When Tris gets home, he looks at the correct answer and has been able to identify and correctly produce the answer! I mean, the teacher is teaching her students!

Tris also learns that friends aren't necessarily friends. Case in point: One "friend" would often take advantage of his generosity by telling Tris he owed him money because he had lost a bet, or race, or something insignificant. Tris handed him a few dollars without thinking twice. This same "friend" then got him into trouble during class by claiming it had been Tris misbehaving. One other time, Tris was in the restroom, located in the portable where he had science with his second science teacher. He was taking a long time, so this kid started banging on the door. The teacher told Tris to get out, but he didn't know was Tris was fixing the toilet, and that he had learned how to by watching it done on the Science Channel!

I said, "Did you *tell* the teacher what you were doing?"

"No, I just wanted Steve to leave me alone, and the toilet needed to be fixed, so I fixed it."

He went on to describe how uncomfortable he was with this teacher because she would tell her class to shut up. Tris has not had a teacher speak to a class in this manner before. He is uncomfortable talking to her.

I spoke to Linda, who knows her. My neighbor

speaks well of her. Tristian is learning how we are all different. I tell him, "You know what? I have found that we all experience rough times when we think no one understands, but I believe that what makes us *different* is how we choose to *handle* those times." Perhaps the teacher is experiencing a rough time of her own. I have met the woman he is speaking of. She is harmless.

My son is accustomed to teachers being kind and respectful to their students. In turn, students are respectful to them. I like it that he has learned good manners! The child he considers his friend possibly has other issues at home that would cause him to behave or misbehave. His sister gets a lot of attention. I tell Tristian, "For all you know, he is just getting attention any way he can."

As far as Tristian is concerned, Steve is just a bully. Bullies want to hurt you because, inside, they are feeling unbearable pain; they can't fix it, so they hurt you. I tell my son, Kill them with kindness. You will catch the bully off guard, and he won't know how to react. That will just show how much wiser you are. My dad gave me this advice as a child.

This has been a transitional year for Tristian. He has to face the FCAT, the Florida Comprehensive Assessment Test. These tests are similar to ones he took at Southwide Academy, but they're oh so different!

Regardless, Tristian scores well on both reading and

math, considering he should be in second grade. He enjoys reading. He doesn't read novels as much as science books. When he is at home, he reads instructions to just about anything. I mean, *anything!* "Mom, your blow dryer has many features you are not using. Or "Let me put the new vacuum together—I'll show you how it works."

I enjoy seeing his mind at work. This year he has been given his first opportunity to do a project for the science fair. Taking advantage of his fascination with batteries, he chooses them as the focus of his project. His uncle has told him to warm batteries after use for optimal use. We have been keeping them in the refrigerator. He decides to test this theory himself. He is given minimal instruction on requirements for the project. He does his own little projects at home anyway. This is fun for him?

We don't even know what the grade was on the project, content only when he passes.

I could have pursued the grade issue, but I am doing my best dealing with my health as well as being a good role model, I hope for Tristian's sake, as he sees Mommy confront her own life battles while remaining positive. It sounds tough to do, and believe me, it is!

So I fall because I am walking when given the chance. But I don't trip and fall, I just slowly find my way closer to the floor! I am as cautious as possible. If

I fall when Tris is home, I say to him, "No big deal" with a smile on my face. I'm really fine, just a little frustrated. I get a little grin from him. I am fully aware of the seriousness of an injury to me. I don't want to frighten or concern him. I want to show him how to handle unexpected times such as these. I quickly make sure I am okay before I tell him, "See? No biggie," as I brush small pieces of fuzz from my clothes. I say to him, "First we make sure no one is hurt, and then we can laugh it off!"

As my child gets older, he is quick to remind me of what I have taught him. I love, love, *love* when he repeats my words to me. I must be doing something right! He even gives me words of encouragement when I question if I can do something. He says firmly," You've done it before. You can do it again."

I'm adjusting to this school as well. It starts much earlier, so I have limited time to exercise prior to getting out of bed. I'm stiff in the morning; my joints are not adjusting to his schedule! It's not just my joints; my body needs a break from it. I have to take care of myself, so I am there for my family. That's how I look at it.

Thankfully, I get assistance from Jim, my physical therapist. He helps me with stretching and exercising, and, even more important, he's taller than I am, so he can easily catch me if I begin to fall! Fortunately, that rarely happens, and he motivates me with the home gym equipment when I just want to stop. He won't let me fatigue.

I'm looking forward to summer so I can get that break. I started using Walk-Aides, a device worn below the knee that sends an electrical current to my feet to assist with drop foot. No drugs! It works for me, not necessarily for others.

I've started to inject myself with copaxone to treat the MS. I'm tolerating the copaxone with methotrexate tablets which I take once a week. Apparently, this med should not interfere with the methotrexate. I'm psyched! I can actually treat both MS and RA! When I start copaxone, I feel fantastic at first, energetic and able to give myself injections daily as ordered. To me, the expensive medication is worth it.

I have spoken to others treating MS with this med. Some have been on it for years.

It doesn't work for long, though. At first, it seemed I was benefiting from it, as evidenced by decreased symptoms, but, eventually, I started to feel worse, not better, following injections. I was dreading the daily shots, because I would feel malaise following them, and no longer felt getting the shots was worth it.

I eventually start taking Ampyra—a tablet taken twice a day to improve walking. It actually works for me, but it does not treat MS, only a single symptom, *walking!* But that's a big deal for me. Many patients are unable to take it because of side effects like balance or seizures. For me, I feel as though I have energy to exercise and make it through each day, hopeful that my attempt to care for this body is going to make treatment, or possibly cure, of these illnesses more likely.

Halloween, October 31, 2009

For Halloween this year, Tristian chose to dress as Albert Einstein. He wore this for school the day they said to dress as someone who had made a difference in the world, like a president, scientist, athlete, etc. He shrugged at the typical Halloween costumes.

May 2010

Promoted to fourth grade! The third grade has been quite challenging at times. I ask Tris, "What did you think of this school compared to the other?"

"It's O.K."

I tell him how proud I am of him as I know change can be difficult for anybody. Whenever we see a staff member from Southwide Academy, whether at church or a store, he doesn't hesitate to ask if the school will be opening again.

August 2010—Fourth Grade

The home room teacher is easy to talk to. I am able to exchange e-mail with her concerning my child. She actually told us the requirements for the science fair.

Science is Tris's favorite subject. He routinely checks out *Popular Science* from the library. This is a large, hardcover book that is dated, but my son manages to find articles of interest for him.

Tris is given numerous opportunities to write stories during an allotted time while in his reading class—unfortunately, not as much time as he thinks he needs!

This becomes a concern for his teacher. Ms. Buntin, his homeroom teacher, is also his reading/writing and science teacher. She tells me he is creative and writes well, but that the work needs to be completed on time. She works on this with me. I mean, she actually works with *me!* I don't feel so isolated handling this situation. Rick and I sign Tris up with Sylvan, to assist him with pulling ideas from his creative head and putting them on paper! He actually enjoys going there. (I think the gifts he is given for productive work might have something to do with it.)

He is promoted to fifth grade.

June 6, 2009

Summer has arrived! How about treating Tristian to a ride on a train to Washington, D.C.? We are all excited about this trip. I am wearing the Walk-Aids on both legs. I will bring them to ambulate as much as possible. Yes, that is the *plan.* Even when sitting, I can turn them on to move my ankles.

We chose to stay in an accessible suite for the two-day, one-night train ride, to help make the trip as tolerable as possible for us (all right, *me*). That consisted of a room with a couch for all three of us to sit on that turned into a bed at night, along with another bed that folded down above it. I was feeling content with the fact that I've been able to live my best with these inconvenient diseases that made their way into my body without conferring with me!

I was looking forward to going there. I have told Tristian how I know he would enjoy the train as I recounted my trip with the safety patrol. I remember how much fun the train ride was with all friends and no parents, and being a patrol at school, making sure kids followed the rules. "It is so *you*, Tristian." I told him how I was a captain for one of the four semesters during my sixth grade. "You will love the train ride and the museums. I know you will love the museums!"

The train ride *was* thrilling for him. We enjoyed it as well. We had our own shower and bathroom; we even had an attendant assisting us when needed. He would turn down the beds at night and we could even dine in the suite if needed to, but we wanted to eat in the dining car! Rick carried me through the tight aisles two cars away. It was tricky, but we were determined! I wanted to walk there, but the train was maybe a little *unsteady?*

The views from the dining car were worth the trouble it had been to get there, though. Sure, I can say that—poor Rick might not be so sure! Hey, at least I'm not heavy.

"Are you having fun, Tristian?"

"Yes!" he exclaims with a big smile on his face.

The train trip was a vacation for Tris and me; Rick enjoyed himself as well but sacrificed the top bed for Tris, and I got the lower one because the beds were small, so Tris and I tried to share, but no way. Rick ended up on the floor! If only he hadn't been facing the bathroom! That's probably not the best way to face on a train while sleeping on the floor. The mattresses were flat and hard, but I doubt they were as hard as the floor for Rick!

The unpleasant odor made for a long night. I am grateful that Rick generously gave up his bed. I believe we were happy to stay in a suite anyhow, all in all. All you need is a disability. On the other hand, though staying in a suite on the train was out of the ordinary for us, *I want to be ordinary.*

We enjoyed our ride. The morning arrived with great anticipation; we gobbled down breakfast in our room and gathered our belongings in anticipation of a great vacation. As we get closer to our destination, we could see the historic buildings we would be visiting. I couldn't wait to get out and stretch. We were all looking forward to stretching and being on stable ground!

It was a beautiful, sunny, *hot* day.

After checking into our hotel, we were pleased to discover we were within walking distance to most attractions.

Our first stop was The National Museum of Natural History. "Wow," Tris said with eyes wide open. He was in heaven, the enormous number of displays completely to his liking. As we made our way through them (with me in the wheelchair while Rick and Tris walked), to our surprise we saw familiar faces in the distance. No way! We looked at each other in disbelief. "Isn't that Eddie and Linda with Tyler and Kelly?" Rick asked.

I looked where he was pointing and nodded. We got their attention and greeted them happily. I told Rick, "We have to get a picture. I told Tris, "Go stand with them!"

After taking the picture, we continued our tour, going our separate ways, knowing we would be leaving to go home days later on the same flight. On vacation at the same place and time with who live right behind us—what a fluke!

The following few days, we enjoyed ourselves by visiting the other museums in unusual weather—from hurricane winds that uprooted trees by the White House to cool, low-humidity, pleasant days. It was those very hot days I found to be the most troublesome. Between the hot weather and always being on the go, I had little time to ambulate. I wore the Walk-Aides daily so as not to miss an opportunity to ambulate while wearing them. When I walk with them on, they keep me from dragging my feet, so I can focus on walking using the proper muscles. Opportunity to ambulate in Washington? Not a chance! Way too many things to see and do! Times like these, I can't wait to go home.

Well, I *almost* ambulated. Almost didn't win football games, though I did it.

2011–2012—Fifth Grade

I can't believe my child is in fifth grade! I can't believe I've made it this far as a mother. I can't believe there is still so much parenting awaiting me for years to come. As I see my son mature into a gentleman, I briefly reflect on my experiences at his age, and I am reminded of how my own mother managed to be there for me during my trivial encounters, which seemed enormous for me. I realize how important it is for me to be available for my son while he confronts many of the same issues most of us face during life. I say this as I observe my own mother continuing to be there for me, always. I wonder what challenges await me and my son as the *planned life* continually takes detours.

This is Tristian's last year in elementary school. We prepare to meet his homeroom teacher. Rick is home today. I am in the wheelchair for the trip. I have already exercised this morning and ambulated, since Rick is home and I feel safe to walk. I am fatigued.

We get to his assigned class room and meet Ms. Bentson. We greet each other, and I place my arm around Tristian, introducing her student to her with a smile on my face. I say, "This is Tristian. He is a good kid."

She fires back, "They are *all* good kids."

I'm immediately concerned for my child. We have already had the privilege of meeting some of the students from the previous years. That's quite a generalization she has come to. Tristian has had to confront bullying, and I specifically asked that Steve be in another class. I nod with a smile, thinking, You are burned out. I feel sympathy for her as she informs me how many years she has been teaching and how she is content she no longer has to teach kindergarteners because they are so needy. I am reminded of nurses I have worked with who are equally burned out, and think, Those kindergarteners' parents must be relieved as well!

I mention how Tristian would enjoy being on safety patrol. She asks him, her head slightly tilted and eyes squinted, "You want to be on patrol?"

He nods cautiously. I can see how uncomfortable he appears. "I'm going to be watching you," she tells him sternly. She is already putting him on the defensive, unaware of how much she will be able to trust, and rely on, this child. I have already had the opportunity, as we have had to deal with our fair share of issues regarding my health as well as bullying.

The year thus starts off stressfully for Tris and me as well. Rick works often, which adds pressure to the entire family, because we are all working but with different goals. Tris wants to make it to middle school; I want to be there for him as he confronts his challenges, but I need to face my health challenges in order to do that. Rick sees co-workers more than us, and that's okay. It's when he gets home that we all get to share his work-related issues. Talk about stress! Maybe this is a good time for family counseling?

I have been aware of Tris's struggles with teachers, homework, and expectations from the beginning. I've asked him randomly, "How is your Homeroom class going?"

He's been brief with his answers.

"Did you hear anything about safety patrol?"

"Yeah, some kids were picked, but there are more to be chosen. They're going, by plane not train, to Washington, D.C.!"

I think, I'm not so sure I want my child flying without his parents—the security X-rays or patting down prior to boarding, the terrorist concerns. . . . I don't know; I'm probably making a big deal out of nothing. If he wants to go to Washington, I am sure he would enjoy being there again. I'm more concerned with the fact that he has not been chosen.

"How do you like Ms. Bentson?" He shrugs, a look of indifference on his face. He says he doesn't understand what he is doing wrong. He says this is her worst class.

"What? Tris, many kids aren't as honest about how they're teachers are speaking to the students. Listen to me. I won't make excuses for her behavior. My main concern is you. She won't be the first teacher that doesn't agree with you."

I ask to speak to her by phone. I'm having trouble understanding her attitude as well. I respectfully listen to her express her concerns as she tells me my child is disruptive and won't behave. What? He tells me he is known as the quiet one by his peers. I'm baffled.

Rick and I set up a conference with all three of his teachers. They are quick to inform us how intelligent he is but easily distracted if the subject is not of interest to him.

I am reminded of his private school teacher telling me how "each student reaches their mental maturity at different times." I think he is mature and responsible, but he is also a boy, which makes it difficult to stay still unless the subject is science!

They continue to tell us they are concerned for middle school because the classes will be double what he has now, so he needs to write in his agenda each day to show he has organized a routine. We agree on a routine for him, with the teachers checking and signing the agenda to show he has been writing in it.

Tris does a biography of Madame Curie for his reading class. When I ask him, "Why did you choose her?" he tells me how his teacher instructed students to pick a book from her selection in the classroom, and that there were only a few left when his turn came, and that, since her Marie Curie is on the poster in his bathroom displaying famous scientists, he chose her. He typed this biography himself, refusing any help from me. It was done so well, it was displayed in the hallway!

March 9, 2012

It is pitch-black in our bedroom, perfect for sleeping! With my eyes scrunched, I barely open them to see the time on the alarm clock. I'm late. My joints are stiff. My whole body is stiff! My muscles need to be reminded of their purpose. All right, I made it through the four-hour night without getting up to use the bathroom. I have thirty minutes to stretch, do a little exercise, and get my tired body out of bed. I'm surprised I wasn't awakened at 4:00 a.m. That's when Rick wakes up to work out in our weight room before leaving for work at 6:00 a.m. It is also when I find myself sitting on the sofa for a few sips of coffee before Tris wakes up with his alarm clock gently beeping. Prior to sitting on the sofa, I have ambulated using a walker with Rick following closely behind me.

I'm still disturbed about Tristian not being chosen for safety patrol, not because he needs to go to Washington, D.C. (he's been there, done that), but because I don't understand how the choices were made. So I call the person in charge of the patrols. She informs me that the homeroom teacher decides. After speaking to Ms. Bentson on the phone, I look at Tris straight in the eyes and tell him, "You know, maybe it's just not meant to be? Everything happens for a reason. I could pursue this, but I'm not sure of why I'd want to. We've already been to Washington, D.C., and had an awesome time. Is this worth it to you?"

"Na, I just want to finish with this school."

He has decided to focus and do his best with encouragement from his parents. He gets "A"s on his report card and does well concentrating on subjects he was having difficulty in. At times, he gets fidgety doing homework. I tell him, "Stop. Get up. Run ten times around the family room and kitchen, then stretch and relax. I am proud of you. You can do this."

I get a snack and tell him, "Take a bite. When you finish your homework, you can eat it all and you can go outside and find something fun to do with your friends."

He is such a good kid. He is content with the plan and agrees.

His hard work pays off as he is chosen to compete in

the District Science Fair. He has the social studies teachers by the end of the year. He has worked so hard. It's time to do something I think he will enjoy. "Do you want to play chess?" I ask him with some hesitation. I haven't played since I played it with Scott. I tell him this as I hand him the instructions; I know he will want to read them first. I tell him how I haven't wanted to play since Scott passed away, but that I believe he will enjoy playing.

He carefully reads the instructions. When he finishes, I say to him, "See? That's what Mathew plays in school. Maybe, once you learn how to play, you and your BFF can play. First, let's play ourselves. . . . It's been a long time for me, you know, and seeing as you just read the instructions, why don't you refresh my memory?"

Without hesitation he does so, and we enjoy playing against each other. He even beats me on occasion!

May 2012

His last math teacher, Ms. Stark, assigns a project for her fifth graders to be completed by the end of the year. It is a difficult, time-consuming, and grueling project given to these children two weeks before graduating elementary school. My son is getting straight "A"s. He works on this project all weekend. He is determined to get an "A". He tells me she is giving *everyone* no higher than a "B".

"No, Tristian, you worked very hard on this. I'm sure, when she sees it, she'll give you whatever you deserve. I don't see a 'B' here. Hopefully, she doesn't either."

He comes home after turning it in and tells me, "Here it is graded." He's received an 80.

"Did she comment on the cover that you worked hard on?"

He shakes his head.

I look through the papers and say, "I don't see any marks to show what is incorrect."

Tris tells me she *told* him she is not giving anyone a higher grade than an 80.

"That doesn't make sense. You deserve a better grade. You worked hard on this project."

I look him in the eyes to see his reaction. He sighs and looks down.

Rick happens to be home, so I tell him, "Look at his project. He did a good job, don't you think?"

He recalls the weekend Tris worked so hard on it. I tell Tris I will talk to the teacher tomorrow.

The next morning, Rick is again home, so we give Tris a ride to school (we don't want him to damage his over-sized cover or papers). As we make our way into the school, he points to the woman walking in front of us and whispers, "That's her."

I am in the wheelchair, barefoot, with the papers in my lap. "Excuse me, Ms. Stark. Hi, I'm Mrs. Capozzi, Tristian's mom." As I hand the papers to her, I comment, "I didn't find marks anywhere to show Tristian what he did incorrectly on this project."

She tells me she will look over the paper and give it back to us today. I get the impression she may not have expected to be questioned about it by a parent.

When Tristian brings the paper home this afternoon, there are still no marks to signify what's wrong with it. "Tristian," I say, "I spoke to her about this, as I told you I would."

He nods in agreement. Rick comments that it *is* nearing the end of the year, so leaving this alone would probably be acceptable.

Later, when I speak to Tris alone, I say as I look into his disappointed eyes, "I can see you're still questioning the grade. I have to admit, so am I, but I am not going to do anything more about it. If it's important to you, you decide what *you* should do. You are a big boy, and this won't be the first time you will be dealing with disagreements with teachers. Confronting her is up to you. If it was me, I would ask myself, 'What's the worst thing that could happen?'"

Raising his eyebrows, he says, "She doesn't talk to me, and my grade stays the same."

I give him a little grin and tell him, "no matter what,

I will support you."

I'm thinking of calling the principal, because she has been helpful to us in the past when I spoke to her about something else, so I believe she would remember us, but I want to wait and see how this works out for Tris. I believe it will build confidence in him.

The next day when he comes home from school, he is practically jumping up and down in excitement. He hands me the project and says, "Look!"

I glance at the sticky note Ms. Stark placed on the front of the paper that reads:

> *Through a conversation w/ Tristian, we were able to go through his project & find items that were not obvious to me. Proud of him for coming to me to fight for his grade.*
>
> Ms. Stark

Ironically, the sticky note has an inscription that reads: *"The future belongs to those who believe in the beauty of their dreams"—Eleanor Roosevelt.*

The grade on his paper has gone from 80 to 98! I give him a great big hug and comment, "Wow, Tristian, I am *so* proud of you! See? That took *guts!* You stood up for what you believed in." I give him another hug and tell him, "See? Good behavior gets rewarded. Now, what can I reward you with?"

I think he was already rewarded with his new grade! Along with receiving his certificate for All Year Honor Roll, he also received The Most Improved and was voted Most Intelligent In The Class. He finishes the year with a graduation that is as entertaining to watch as a Broadway musical! The boys dressed in their black slacks with a white button-down shirt and a tie of their choosing. The girls wore beautiful white dresses that they had chosen as well. Each child approached the principal to receive his or her diploma.

Once the diplomas were handed to each child, it was time to recognize students for exceptional performance. When Tris's class was announced, Tris was the only one in his class to receive the Gold Presidential Award for Academic Excellence!

I felt honored to be his mother. I am sure Rick was as well to be his dad.

Rick had helped me out of my wheelchair, so I was able to sit in one of the auditorium seats along with him and my parents.

The children were all on the stage for their finale. They each put on sunglasses that had previously been given to them; then they left the stage quickly and in an orderly, single file to the song "That's What Makes You Beautiful" by One Direction. This song is even more meaningful to me, because when we heard it on the radio, I told Tris I liked it, and he pointed out the lyrics, "You don't know you're beautiful / That's what makes you beautiful." I told him how awesome he was to recognize I needed to hear something as simple as that, and I reminded him of how I was lucky to have a beautiful child like him. I got back in the wheelchair after the kids left the stage.

Once we left the building, Ms. Bentson approached me to say, "What do you think about that?" smiling as she nodded.

I smiled back, thinking, You just found out what I've been telling you from the first day I met you!

WRAPPING UP

I've done it, numb left pinky and all.

I said I wished there was a book to guide me through life, and instead of just wishing it, I did it!

I'm not an author; I'm an average human being. Gosh, that feels good to say! Even as I typed slowly with my clumsy hands, I've proved to myself that nothing is impossible. I am aware of the voice-activated program that would type my words for me, and I know I could easily have asked someone to type them for me, but what an awesome feeling I get to have accomplished it on my own! I've even made sure the words are larger, to help those of us who have trouble reading small print . . . like *me*. As I sacrificed my time to exercise and move, it was important to me that I finish this book, because I told Tristian I would jot down words that have helped me during tough times, so maybe they could assist him during his life.

I feel our quality of life is ultimately determined by

choices we make. Many times I have not been in control of situations I experienced, whether through abuse as an innocent child or adult, or diagnosed with diseases that have no cure; I have decided, however, to take back that which I *can* control and live my life to the best of my ability. I choose not to give abusers control of *me*. I can do that by choosing to let go of those memories and take back the part of me they have stolen. No more stealing my life! I'm in control now. As far as living with chronic incurable diseases, there are many choices I am in control of as well, such as the medication I take, the amount of exercise I decide to do, and my behavior as I make those choices.

I believe that, as human beings, we are all more alike than we are different. I want my son to see the glass half full, not half empty. I keep referring to my son, because as far as I'm concerned, his generation is our future. I've had my time to live during each age he has passed through. I feel it is up to me to show and teach him what I have learned during *my* life so far.

This is what I have learned.

I have discovered how important it is to be optimistic. A pessimist is rarely welcomed.

I have learned how influential my opinion can be. Through experiences I have encountered, I've learned of the power of a smile. I am struggling to live my life as close to normal as possible during my fight with illness.

I have discovered that the friend I am searching for has been with me all along. That friend is me. I am able to communicate with this friend through my journal, just as my sister said. It is always there for me.

By caring about myself, I show others I'm worth caring about. Everyone is worth caring about. While watching someone being treated unfairly—that would be *me*, the one who is doing her best to function with this physical body while my spiritual self is healthy and thriving. As such, I can display survival to the best of my ability. I inform our family counselor that the physical me is a mess but the spiritual me is strong. This is *my* life.

Oh, as I complete my writing, I am reminded of what Raul told me on December 26, 1981. I would tell him if he was still alive, "*No lo perdi,*" which means "I didn't lose it." This life thing is *all about attitude!*

Remember:
- You are in charge of your life, which is shaped by choices *you make.*
- Don't just wish it, do it!
- Negative energy is wasted energy, counterproductive.
- Treat others the way you want to be treated.
- Trust yourself (nobody knows you better than you).
- Expectations can lead to disappointment.
- It's always easy to do the wrong thing.

- It's always harder to do the right thing.
- Depression is anger turned inward.
- People see you as you see yourself.
- Life is *not* fair.
- Avoid doing something you will regret doing!
- We often hate what we don't understand.
- Live today as if it was your last.
- People treat you the way you *let* them
- Ask yourself, "What advice would I give to someone I care about?" Follow your own advice!
- One person *can* make a difference.
- Words are powerful.
- It's not what problems we have; it's how we confront them.
- Everything happens for a reason.
- You can laugh, or you can cry.
- Love is when you feel good about yourself when you are with a person (i.e., "I love the way I look through your eyes.")
- Gossip is unattractive behavior and a waste of good energy!
- Hypocrisy is exercised by those who should be working on their own problems.
- Almost won a football game? Tell the Miami Dolphins—they've almost won several.
- Have faith in a higher power: Life is difficult on your own.

- Don't just pray for a cure but for strength to handle whatever comes your way.
- Focus, meditate: It does a body good.
- Mistakes are there to learn from, not repeat!
- Money: It's not how much you have, it's what you *do* with it.
- Bullies: They want to hurt you because, inside, they are feeling unbearable pain that they can't deal with, so they want you to hurt too.
- Kill them with kindness.
- Smiles are contagious.

Tristian and me